THE ALIENATION OF FACT

THE ALIENATION OF FACT

Digital Educational Privatization, AI, and the False Promise of Bodies and Numbers

Kenneth J. Saltman

The MIT Press
Cambridge, Massachusetts
London, England

The MIT Press would like to thank the anonymous peer reviewers who provided comments on drafts of this book. The generous work of academic experts is essential for establishing the authority and quality of our publications. We acknowledge with gratitude the contributions of these otherwise uncredited readers.

This book was set in Stone Serif by Westchester Publishing Services. Printed and bound in the United States of America.

Library of Congress Cataloging-in-Publication Data is available.

Names: Saltman, Kenneth J., 1969– author.
Title: The alienation of fact : digital educational privatization, AI, and the false promise of bodies and numbers / Kenneth J. Saltman.
Description: Cambridge, Massachusetts : The MIT Press, [2022] | Includes bibliographical references and index.
Identifiers: LCCN 2022005023 (print) | LCCN 2022005024 (ebook) | ISBN 9780262544368 (Paperback) | ISBN 9780262371735 (PDF) | ISBN 9780262371742 (ePub)
Subjects: LCSH: Artificial intelligence—Educational applications. | Privatization in education. | Verification (Empiricism)
Classification: LCC LB1028.43 .S26 2022 (print) | LCC LB1028.43 (ebook) | DDC 370.285—dc23/eng/20220608
LC record available at https://lccn.loc.gov/2022005023
LC ebook record available at https://lccn.loc.gov/2022005024

10 9 8 7 6 5 4 3 2 1

CONTENTS

PREFACE

Economic inequality, the devastation of global warming, the threat of nuclear annihilation, and the failure of politics to address these existential threats drives material and symbolic precarity.[1] Growing material precarity is amplified by crises in a number of symbolic domains that have traditionally provided people the means to act on and shape their social world. News media is beset by crises of credibility as digital manipulation, social media takeover, and corporate media consolidation have resulted in commercial content and punditry replacing journalism, while rising authoritarian leaders aim to discredit journalism.[2] Following 40 years of neoliberal hegemony, liberal electoral politics faces a crisis of legitimacy, as it appears to have failed to provide citizens with the means to effect policy. While policy influence is vast for ruling class citizens, most citizens and mass-based interest groups have little or no influence.[3] This crisis of legitimacy is amplified by authoritarian politicians and political parties hellbent on discrediting electoral democracy.[4] Neoliberal ideology itself faces a crisis of legitimacy amid vastly worsening economic inequality; declining mobility; and soured promises of markets, jobs, and consumption.[5] The outcome of neoliberal privatization, deregulation, financialization, and evisceration of the social state has been realized in radical material precarity: a mere 1 percent of the world's population

owns more than half of all the wealth, and the top 20 percent owns 94.5 percent, leaving 80 percent of the global population with only 4.5 percent.[6] The pandemic amplified this
extreme class inequality: trillions of dollars bailed out corporations, and the 600 richest billionaires increased their wealth
by $700 billion, while 50 million US workers lost their jobs.[7]
Neoliberal culture should be radically discredited. Prior to the
pandemic, education faced crises of credibility as decades of
systemic defunding and privatizations were paired with anti-
intellectual, anti-critical, and punitive test and accountability
regimes.[8] Rather than providing the means to interpret and act
on the world, education has been eroded through instrumental-
ism, vocationalism, and the expansion of repressive pedagogies
propelled by the neoliberal privatization and accountability
movements.[9]

In the face of material and symbolic precarity and the erosion of the traditional mechanisms for individual and collective agency, people grasp for certainty. To be clear, journalism,
politics, and education have been systematically undermined
as instruments of collective action and self-governance. Growing inequality, precarity, and crises of agency have caused
many people to succumb to the assurance of certainty offered
by fundamentalisms and authoritarianism.[10] Fundamentalist
religion and market fundamentalism provide false guarantees of certainty grounded in dogma. Authoritarian leaders
promise false security in exchange for an abdication of liberty.
Around the world, Strongmen[11] mystify the causes of inequality; scapegoat the vulnerable; attack science, education, and
truth; and offer themselves up as identifications with strength.
The swindle of authoritarianism depends on a false guarantee
of security and certainty. This book details a pattern. In the
face of precarity, insecurity, and the erosion of the traditional
forms of agency, people are desperately grasping for foundations in forms that falsely appeal to concreteness: numbers
and bodies.

The turn to the false foundational guarantees of numbers and bodies can be found across institutions and fields. As digital technology amplifies audit culture[12] and corporate logic, the quantification and datafication of the natural and social worlds permeate everything from policing to the humanities and education at every level. The fetish for metrics promoted by the ideologies of industrial efficiency, scientific management, and positivism are hardly new. But the business of data tech—artificial intelligence (AI), predictive analytics, the Internet of Things, adaptive learning technologies, and data commerce—and neoliberal ideology amplify the crucial contemporary contradiction around fact. That is, on one hand, everything must be measured, quantified, and subject to data analytics; and on the other hand, every domain is facing a crisis of truth and legitimacy in which facts appear to be free-floating, ungrounded, and arbitrary. Politicians and news venues eschew science, expertise, and education, instead blurting assertions without evidence, argument, or theoretical justification. The refusal of evidence, argument, and theory has become stunningly mainstream. Most Republican voters deem higher education to be "bad for America";[13] only 27 percent of Republicans trust scientists, and only 31 percent trust medical science.[14] Following the 2020 presidential election, 70 percent of Republicans believed Donald Trump's incessantly repeated lies that the 2020 election were "rigged" and "fraudulent" despite the lack of evidence, and as of 2019, 130 members of Congress denied human-caused global warming. A growing number of people embrace outlandish conspiracy theories, with the least educated being the most vulnerable to believing them (I discuss this phenomenon in chapters 5 and 6).[15]

In education, this contradiction around fact appears omnipresent—everything must be "data driven," and yet policy proceeds free of evidence, argument, or theoretical justification. The misrepresentation of learning as quantifiable test outcomes continues in both traditional and new high-tech

forms. Affect and behavior must now be quantifiably measured, and the body comes increasingly to be rendered as data.
Online education platforms, biometric pedagogy and surveillance devices, adaptive learning technologies, and avatars for
social and emotional learning are just some of the growing
data-generating industries involved in for-profit contracting.
Yet policies—particularly market-based ones like chartering,
vouchers, and these innumerable tech platforms—expand
without evidence for their efficacy or adequate theoretical justifications.[16] I call this contradiction between the imperative
for data and the evacuation of argument, evidence, and theory
"the alienation of fact." Increasingly, claims about essentialized others and their bodies and decontextualized numbers
ground assertions of truth in place of argument and evidence.
This book aims to make sense of this contradiction, particularly as it has been brought about in part by destructive trends
in public schooling.

The chapters of this book illustrate the alienation of fact
through different cases and different educational domains:
from AI education to The LEGO Group's quantification of
play, from the digitalization of social and emotional learning
to the privatized corporeal politics of biometric pedagogy, safe
spaces, affinity groups, and rampant conspiracy theories. The
false promise of control in manipulating data and manipulating bodies turns the pursuit of rational progress into a frenzy
of irrationalism.[17] For example, social and emotional learning
apps "cure" social alienation not by engaging children in dialogue about their experiences and how their experiences are
produced socially but by putting children in front of screens to
be socialized en masse by AI avatars. Perhaps no more recent
glaring example of the alienation of fact has appeared than
in the COVID-19 pandemic response by certain outspoken
advocates of educational privatization. As public schools were
closed across the United States to stop the spread of the virus,
districts and states turned to online learning. Children whose

parents are advised by the American Academy of Pediatricians to limit screen time to 2 hours per day were put in front of screens for 8 hours. As technology companies cashed in on contracting arrangements with districts and saw their stock prices skyrocket, school districts opted to keep children indoors and in front of computers. Rather than taking schooling outdoors (where the virus spread is nearly zero, and learning could be socially contextualized, socially interactive, and engaged with nature and the built environment), learning became a radically private and intensely alienated affair of online education oriented around decontextualized, mass-produced, homogenous, corporate curriculum. Control over bodies and the measurement of those bodies using data and metrics is prioritized. Nearly all US schools closed in the spring of 2020 with the majority turning to a small number of remote learning apps, such as Google Classroom and a variety of commercial apps. During the pandemic, Google Classroom jumped from 40 million to 150 million users globally, and Zoom was used by 125,000 schools in 25 countries.[18]

At the outset of the pandemic, leading scholars of educational technology, such as Ben Williamson, and the journal *Learning Media and Technology* warned that much needed to be studied before jumping to conclusions about the implications of widespread online education.[19] Yet before the implications of such a radical change to school practice could be studied, long-time education privatization advocates, such as Bill Gates and Andrew Cuomo, announced the end of brick and mortar schooling and the "reimagining" of schooling as online education—essentially the handing over of the public education system to private technology companies.[20] In a short time, the failure of fully online schooling in the elementary grades became clear, as students reported headaches and fatigue, and in Chicago alone tens of thousands of students signed a petition rejecting the format. The fetish for control of data, information, and the body, the interest in technology profits, and the promotion of techno-utopian ideology aligned with a longstanding neoliberal privatization agenda and the prioritization of the consumption of decontextualized, standardized lessons. Data production, accumulation, and crunching were of paramount importance in decision making about how to do school in a pandemic. Yet the policy of putting children in front of screens all day for what has been a largely transmissional mode of pedagogy was not backed by medical science, pedagogical research, or any other rational argument or evidence. Unsurprisingly, market fundamentalist think tanks, including the American Enterprise Institute, Heritage Foundation, and Hoover Institution, put out advocacy reports during the pandemic without supporting research. These reports called for vast expansion of vouchers and neovoucher scholarship tax credits to fund for-profit cyber microschools and Airbnb-style online education brokers that connect private instructors with parents.[21] These reports admit that such schemes are racially and economically exclusionary yet call for privatizations (proven to exacerbate educational inequality, segregation, and funding disparities)[22] to expand them. During the pandemic, the dropout recovery agency Graduation Alliance, owned by global investment firm KKR, made millions in contracts with multiple states doing telemarketing robocalls to students. The company counted these calls as successful interventions and sold their services despite a lack of evidence for efficacy.[23] In place of evidence, argument, or theory, the basis of policy was faith—a longstanding faith in markets and a faith in techno-utopian progress expressed through technology contracting and the vast new educational business in capturing student energy to produce economically valuable data.[24] What was squandered was an opportunity at best for learning to be contextualized, meaningful, and related to student experience, and for such meaningful learning to become the basis for self-understanding and social intervention. At least what was squandered was an opportunity for children to play, imagine, read, and have time off of the productivist treadmill of "academic gains" that treats learning as following a fixed, linear direction that progresses with the rise of state standards. Subsequent research has painted a damning picture of online learning during the pandemic.[25] Meanwhile, in the United States, the COVID-19 case numbers illustrated in charts and graphs represented sick and dead bodies standing in for a missing concerted plan or policy to control the virus—testing, tracking, and quarantining that succeeded in numerous nations. The only agency provided to most citizens was the consumption of data about the casualties while the federal government under Trump largely abdicated responsibility for a coordinated response in the name of market fundamentalism—reopening and getting back to business.

This book aims to make sense of a puzzling phenomenon. If there is an imperative for data collection, data-based decision making, empiricist turns in the humanities and social sciences, and the expansion of data science to all social realms, why is there also a flagrant and seemingly growing disregard for fact, evidence, and truth? I provide a few answers in this book. I argue that the very turn to decontextualized data as truth revives and reworks the culture of positivism and carries with it a disregard for the assumptions, values, ideologies, and theories that undergird truth claims.[26] Following Adorno, I contend that the evacuation of theory and fetishization of decontextualized fact expand in a context of not just precarious social conditions and radical inequality but also of market exchange. All things become ephemeral as their meaning is translated into abstract exchange value, leaving people desperately seeking for certainty, concreteness, and foundations.[27] The rendering of all things not just into abstract markers of monetary exchange but also into abstract units of data produces an allure for the concrete, the material, the certain, and the secure. In place of argument, evidence, and theory, in such a context, bodies and numbers provide a particular attraction.

As part of the alienation of fact, conspiracy theory explains social events not through social theory and the dialectical interplay of social structure and agency but through the inexplicable workings of salvational strongman superagents endowed with a mystical capacity to move history and conspiratorial secret agents—minorities and women—conspiring to corporeally replace white Christian men.

Rising authoritarianism depends on an attack on truth. Donald Trump, Viktor Orban, Rodrigo Duterte, Vladimir Putin, Jair Bolsonaro, Abdel Fattah el-Sisi, Recep Tayyan Erdogan, Narendra Modi, and Benjamin Netanyahu, to name a few authoritarians, have undermined knowledge-making institutions, including schools and universities, news media outlets and journalists, and venues for free expression. They seek to delegitimate the very possibility of knowing, so that knowledge is equated with authority and truth resides in the strongman. In this book, I argue that the legacies of positivism in mainstream education, news, and corporate media contribute to and have been a precondition for the crisis of truth that drives the popular turn toward authoritarian leaders. These trends in the realm of culture and politics need to be understood in relation to broader political economic tendencies driving the alienation of fact.

Globally the transnational capitalist class promotes a public education agenda that furthers its economic interests and cultural-political dominance. Around the world, ruling class people and the organizations that represent them largely aim to transform public education itself into private industry and capture the purpose and use of public education for private sector profit through labor training, commercialism, and the reproduction of the social relations for capital accumulation. This agenda is being pursued in a number of ways and by different kinds of organizations. The chapters in this book recount the historical ways that business and ruling class people have sought to profit from public education. They also address what is new and different through a discussion of some of the initiatives championed by supranational organizations, corporations, corporate foundations, superrich individuals, and elite institutions (such as universities, nonprofit foundations, and nongovernmental organizations). Among the new trends in educational privatization are stealth privatizations (such as impact investing and its convergence with the quantification of affect, behavior, and care as part of the new prominent role of digital technology), AI, and datafication in the private sector capture of public education. Recently, the so-called "soft skills" of student behavior and affect in public schools have become the objects for measurement and quantification.

During the industrial era, public education contributed to social and cultural reproduction of capital largely through the long-term investment in workers slated for their place in the production process. Capital in the industrial era used public education largely for teaching skills and know-how necessary for work ideologically conducive to social relations of production.[28] The principle means of profit was realized through creating the conditions for labor exploitation. The culture of positivism that falsely presented knowledge as universally valuable, neutral, and apolitical largely served to conceal the capitalist basis for public schooling—what critical sociologists termed the "hidden curriculum."[29] During the neoliberal era from the early 1980s to the present, ruling class uses of public education shifted. Public schools still reproduced the racialized class hierarchy by teaching working class and poor students basic skills for work as well as teaching professional class students knowledge and ideology conducive to leadership roles in the public and private sectors. However, during the neoliberal era, schools have been re-imagined as business, students and parents as consumers, and knowledge as a commodity to be efficiently or inefficiently delivered. Schools were made into businesses for direct profit extraction in the form of contracting and commercialism initiatives, like advertising in textbooks and sponsorship arrangements, for-profit charter schools, voucher schemes, and scholarship tax credits that function like vouchers. In addition, various real estate and bond investment schemes were created through nonprofit chartering.

The neoliberal era has featured a pronounced hangover of the industrial era's focus on quantifiable efficiency, industrial style accountability, and ever greater levels of control. The standards and accountability movement pushed high stakes standardized testing, the standardization of curriculum, and an intensified "banking education" model.[30] While the hidden curriculum of capitalism was now an overt agenda, positivism continued to play a pronounced role in the centrality of testing and curricular standardization. The denial of the politics of knowledge was integral to the growing multibillion-dollar industry in testing and textbook publishing, homogenization, standardization, and economies of scale to maximize profit. What characterized these control-oriented reforms was not only the predominance of ideologies of industrial efficiency, corporate culture, and consumerism but also greater degrees of repressive control over time, space, and students' bodies. This was readily apparent in for-profit charter schools, such as Edison Learning, where the curriculum and pedagogy were standardized and homogenized for all students in the same grade across all schools in the United States. At KIPP, Inc. (Knowledge is Power Program) schools, grit-oriented pedagogies of control revived behaviorist strategies of teaching.

Meanwhile, as the most aggressively market-oriented reforms targeted the poorest, black and brown schools in the United States, they also imposed rigid, disciplinary, and highly standardized approaches to teaching paired with prison-like and militarized space and technology aimed at instilling strict obedience to authority and controlling bodies. Professional class schools, while also subject to anticritical anti-intellectual heavy testing, positioned students as entrepreneurial subjects of capacity who needed to learn to manage themselves and their bodies for exclusionary competition. Such competition involved learning to self-administer the tools of self-capacity, such as anti-anxiety and attention drugs.

For both working class and poor students as well as professional class students, the learned self-regulation of the industrial era gave way to more direct forms of corporeal control. Twenty years ago, I named the convergence of corporatization and repression in education "Education as Enforcement." The demise of ideological alternatives to neoliberal dominance in the discourse of globalization made liberal politics paired with capitalist economics the only game in town, and the purpose of education was to enforce allegedly apolitical knowledge and to champion a falsely disinterested managerialism. "Education as Enforcement," the expansion of educational repression, has a decidedly economic dimension. What William I. Robinson calls "militarized accumulation" refers to the ways that, in the context of the thorough saturation of commercial exploitation everywhere, ongoing crises of overaccumulation, and crises of political legitimation, capital resorts to force in order to extract value from the aspects of the lifeworld that have yet to be subject to the logic of capital.[31] One of the more obvious examples of this in education include the extent to which privatization initiatives like charters typically are paired with repressive pedagogies and disciplinary tactics to expel students from the private into the public schools. Another example is the drugging of kids into test score performance, where pharmaceutical and test and textbook publishing companies make billions of dollars from the implementation of high-stakes standardized testing paired with epidemic ADHD diagnoses. Perhaps the most obvious form of this is the use of natural and human made disasters to impose vast privatization schemes, as has been done in New Orleans, Detroit, Puerto Rico, and post-invasion Iraq as well as many other places.

Militarized accumulation also occurs as the growing attention to and targeting of student "soft skills" of affect and emotion increasingly has become the focus of neoliberal human capital proponents.[32] Efforts to quantify social emotional learning and play are new. Moreover, the quantification is being developed in conjunction with commercial digital technologies, such as AI, blockchain, and the Internet of Things. The quantification of social behavior and affect is promoted by a rapidly expanding industry in impact investing. Impact investors aim to allow public–private partnerships (that is, privatization of public services). Impact investors aim to quantify social life and the natural world to make every imaginable thing into an investment security under the guise of accountability, cost savings, and corporate social responsibility.[33] As this book makes clear, what is afoot is a convergence of impact investing schemes, philanthrocapitalism that redefines profit seeking as charity, and the quantification of human affect and behavior to legitimate global standards of affect and behavior and to legitimate forcing children to produce commercially valuable data under the guise of care, human development, and progress. This book also makes clear that the human costs of continuing to deny the politics of knowledge and theory and to embrace a false universality are far more dangerous than is commonly acknowledged. Democracy depends on the capacity for public dialogue, debate, and dissent and on the tools to interpret and judge claims to truth. That is, citizens need the intellectual and political tools to comprehend how facts are undergirded by values, assumptions, and ideologies. The chapters that follow make the case that in response to the reactionary educational conditions that have fostered the alienation of fact, the tradition of critical pedagogy provides the tools to produce democratic forms of identification and public life.

In what follows, each chapter does three things. First, each examines a different dimension of the alienation of fact—how bodies and numbers are providing false foundations and a false promise of security and certainty in place of evidence, argument, and theory. That is, each chapter deals with the resurgence of essentialized subjectivity or the resurgence and new uses of positivist ideology in the new terrain of digital educational privatization, or both. Second, each chapter explains these foundational promises in terms of new expressions of the privatization of the public sphere. The chapters analyze digital forms of educational privatization and the privatization of public culture. Third, each chapter contrasts the possibilities of critical pedagogy with the alienation of fact and the new and ongoing directions of educational privatization. Here, as in other work, I hope to expand the scope of critical pedagogy as an engagement with educational politics and policy and a struggle for education to contribute to a more democratic and just society.

Chapter 1 explains the alienation of fact through the changing legacies and functions of positivist education in the industrial, postindustrial, and digital economies. It explains the implication of neoliberal restructuring of education, its accountability and standards movement, and the corporatization of journalism in contributing to the conditions for the crisis of truth and the turn against theory and interpretation as well as evidence and expertise. The chapter explains how educational privatization and corporate media consolidation have contributed to rising authoritarianism through the framing of knowledge. Positivist reforms (such as high stakes standardized testing, teaching to tests, and curricular standardization), have promoted an approach to learning and knowledge in which truth has been aligned with unquestionable authority and rendered a matter of faith and dogma.

Chapter 2 details the new digital privatization as typified in the varieties of AI education—adaptive learning, biometrics, and the convergence of digital surveillance and data commerce with impact investment schemes. AI education is sold based on the false promises of personalization, attention to context and culture, and a reduction of standardized testing. Digital privatization brings together the false promises of essentialized bodies and the positivist fetish for quantification. For example, biometric pedagogy measures bodies; frames teaching as a biological effect; and removes thinking, dialogue, and mediation from the process of teaching and learning. Under the guise of overcoming excessive testing and personalization, adaptive learning builds the pedagogy around constant testing and promotes decontextualized, depersonalized approaches to teaching while creating a new "techno tracking": sorting and sifting students while obscuring the cultural politics of knowledge and the unequal distribution of cultural capital. This chapter also argues that data in educational technology needs to be comprehended as a form of representational politics. It illustrates the emancipatory potential in AI education with the example of a public pedagogy, Forensic Architecture's "Triple Chaser" project, that undoes counters the alienation of facts about weapons by revealing their often hidden producers, users, and victims across geography.

Chapter 3 examines the growing intersections of for-profit digital educational apps and the growing discourse of social and emotional learning (SEL). For-profit SEL programs, including surveillance tracking apps and AI avatars, are being employed to regulate and control students' bodies and teach self-management of emotions. I argue that these technologies measure, quantify, datafy, and normalize behavior and affect while making student activity into data manufacture. In addition, this chapter details how the SEL agenda has been integrated into the human capital model of supranational organizations that aim to yoke public education to the service of business through both digital commerce and affective and corporeal control.

Chapter 4 details how the world's largest toy manufacturer, LEGO Group, has, through the LEGO Foundation, sought to quantify play to make play-based learning part of global standards through the Organisation of Economic Co-operation and

Development, thereby creating the conditions for the global consumption of their products to be understood as necessary to human development and educational improvement. The quantification of play also serves the expansion of LEGO into digital and data commerce with the interface between plastic toys and screens. The chapter details how LEGO has sought to redefine play, creativity, and imagination through work and a skills-based career and technical education privatization agenda. I detail how this reframing misappropriates key critical and progressive education concepts.

Chapter 5 explains the educational conditions for rising conspiracy theory. It shows how the recent vast expansion of conspiracy theories results in part from the ways that the relationship between subjectivity and agency has been redefined by neoliberal educational restructuring and mass media. As knowledge becomes a decontextualized commodity in the current culture of positivism, agency becomes mystified and comprehended through essentialized subjects: salvational superagents (such as Strongmen) and sinister secret agents (such as scapegoated minorities).

Chapter 6 considers how crises of hegemony and agency drive the growing distrust of expertise and specialization. The chapter shows how doubt about the guise of objectivity in education and journalism is being directed to a reactionary politics of paranoia, scapegoating, and hatred as well as to a liberal doubling down on the guise of disinterested objectivity that depoliticizes knowledge and denies cultural politics. The chapter builds on chapters 3 and 4 to examine educational technology projects that merge data commerce with the new quasi-science of affect in terms of the growing distrust of science and expertise. It also challenges depoliticized interpretations of these trends. The chapter argues for approaches to expertise, specialization, and knowledge that foster critical consciousness and healthy doubt about the relationships between truth claims and authority.

Chapter 7 concerns the false promise of certainty located in the body. It succinctly examines how essentialized subjectivity plays out on K–12 and university campuses and online with "virtue signaling," "safe spaces," and "affinity groups." It revisits debates about racial essentialism and whiteness from the 1990s to argue that struggles for democratic education and antiracism need to reject grounding politics in the essentialized body in ways that conflate ideology with identity and in liberal guilt. This chapter contends that the personalization and corporealization of politics spreading in schools, on campus, and online represent a dangerous flight from the public sphere and an inadvertent fueling of reactionary politics rather than fostering antiracist pedagogies as part of radically democratic commitments. The conclusion calls for critical pedagogical projects aligned with social movements to challenge the alienation of fact and to expand the democratic and emancipatory potential of public schooling and educational institutions.

ACKNOWLEDGMENTS

I thank MIT Press editor Susan Buckley for her insights and advice on the development of this project. Robin Truth Goodman once again discussed with me and provided crucial feedback on every chapter. I cannot thank her enough for her brilliance and generosity. I also want to express my great appreciation to Alex Means who also had an outsized impact on this project through conversations and suggestions for reading. A number of colleagues and friends informed this project through dialogue and support including Henry Giroux, Jeffrey Di Leo, Donaldo Macedo, Nicole Nguyen, Enora Brown, Mark Garrison, David Hursh, Ben Superfine, Marc Van Overbeke, Kathryn Chval, Pauline Lipman, Graham Slater and the participants of the Society for Critical Exchange Winter Theory Institute. I am grateful to my new colleagues at UIC for their welcome and support and I appreciate the thoughtful dialogue and exchange with my students. A special shout out to friends Brian Kremen and Liz Hilt of Chicago's only bicycle and knitting store Cog Cycles and Yarns. Their bikes provided a needed antidote to confined quarters during the pandemic and have transformed my experience of Chicago. Thanks as well to loved ones and friends Kathy Szybist, Simone Saltman, Kevin Bunka, Al Lingis, Chris Murray, Noah Gelfand, and Rob Isaacs. A dear friend Jeff Truell died as I was finishing this book. He is missed. I so appreciate his friendship, humor, warmth, and kindness—traits that will continue to resonate in those of us fortunate to have known him. I thank Bloomsbury and the editors for permission to reprint a version of chapter one which appeared as "Antitheory, Positivism, and Critical Pedagogy" in (ed. Jeffrey Di Leo) *What's Wrong with Anti-Theory* New York: Bloomsbury 2019. I thank the editors of *Symploke* for permission to reprint an earlier version of chapter five which appeared as "Salvational Super-Agents and Conspiratorial Secret Agents: Conspiracy, Theory, and Fantasies of Control" *Symploke* 28 (1–2), 51–63 and part of chapter seven which appeared as "Privilege Checking, Virtue Signaling, and Safe Spaces: What Happens When Cultural Politics is Privatized and the Body Replaces Argument" *Symploke* 26 (1–2), 403–409.

1 THE ALIENATION OF FACT: ANTITHEORY, POSITIVISM, AND CRITICAL PEDAGOGY

Across social institutions, an imperative for positivism demands data accumulation, data display, data-driven leadership, and data-driven accountability regimes. In the tradition of positivist rationality, facts are alienated from the conditions of their production and appear to speak for themselves, to be meaningful on their own, requiring no interpretation. A number of fields have succumbed to data-driven rhetoric. Police departments use CompStat to aggregate and crunch crime statistics and then orient their policing activities to "juke the stats." Journalism remains bound to the guise of disinterested objectivity. Perhaps more than any other field, the imperative for positivism pervades education. Public schooling uses test-based accountability, in which learning is equated with numerical test scores, and changes to teaching and administrative practice are to be guided by the numerical outcomes. Superintendents, principals, and teachers are, according to educational rhetoric and doxa, to be driven not by theorizing educational situations but rather by data. Data-driven discourse presumes that the data is not collected with underlying theoretical assumptions or interpreted by such assumptions.

The leading educational policies pertaining to teacher education accreditation (Council for the Accreditation of Educator Preparation), student-teaching assessment (Pearson-run edTPA), and curriculum (the Common Core State Standards) largely assume that knowledge is a deliverable commodity, teachers are delivery agents, and students are knowledge consumers. These policies share an approach to learning and knowledge characterized by an active denial of how knowledge relates to the experience and subjectivity of students and teachers. In addition, these policies fail to recognize the ways that learning and knowledge relate to the world and the capacity of subjects to use knowledge to shape it. These dominant educational policies presume a conception of agency in which the social power of the individual derives from the acquisition and exchange of socially consecrated knowledge. Agency in this view does not derive from the use of knowledge to interpret, judge, act on, and shape the social world while reflecting on what one does. Instead, agency appears as consumption and display of knowledge for academic promotion and later material consumption.

The expansion of radical empiricism coincides with a crisis of truth, evidence, knowledge, information, and education. This crisis of truth appears in educational discourse as specifically market-based educational policy, and practices are promoted and implemented regardless of a lack of evidence for them or even despite counterevidence. For example, vouchers, charters, school turnarounds, and urban portfolio models are all privatization schemes that are unsupported by empirical evidence, are undermined by empirical evidence, or for which empirical evidence is impossible to obtain.[1] Nonetheless, all of these schemes are promoted by rightist think tanks. In the United States, Departments of Education under both parties have embraced unsubstantiated policies swayed by advocacy organizations. Both conservative and liberal think tanks largely adhere to the radical empiricist model, bickering in policy briefs over numbers and measurement methodologies and seldom going beyond disputes over efficacy. For example, do charter schools raise or lower test scores? The focus on positivist measures of numerical efficacy elides questions about the economic, political, and cultural purposes and roles of schooling. Implicit in the efficacy debates is an assumption that schools assimilate people for the existing social order—that is, they make productive future workers and citizens who will accept electoral republican democracy in its corporate-managed form—rather than learning to transform society in more just, equal, and free ways.

Similarly, value-added modeling seeks to replace the tradition of rewarding teacher experience with pay for test outcomes. Value-added modeling calls for K–12 administrators to measure teacher performance by standardized test outputs and links compensation and job security to the numbers. Universities defund the interpretive humanities and expand fields not just with commercial application but also with empirical orientation, while theory is replaced by a resurgent archival research and emphasis on data collection. Higher education is regularly being subject to calls for quantifying student learning through tests and then tying financing to the outputs. Student income loans make this explicit, as private tuition lending is tied to the expected future earnings of the student. Under the pretext of consumer protection from the predatory for-profit higher education sector, The US Department of Education under Obama began measuring the value of universities based on the future earnings of students relative to the costs of the education. Of course, these projects belie not only an instrumental rationality, in which interpretive forms of learning have no place, they also lend themselves to being linked to commercial exchange and commercial competition. These assumptions became more overt under the Trump administration's educational initiatives, which included aggressive promotion of for-profit education at all levels.

This chapter explains the central role of radical empiricism and the hostility to theory in education and journalism. In the contemporary crisis of truth, in place of theory, argument, and evidence, people are seeking foundations for assertion in forms that offer a false promise of certainty—numbers and human bodies. I focus on the contradiction between the simultaneous *faith in fact* for public, academic, and policy discourse and the widespread *disregard for fact*, evidence, argument, and truth in these domains. The first section in this chapter takes up this contradiction in education historically and at present. The second section addresses journalism, and the third discusses how both education and journalism can be understood as the alienation of fact: the replacement of fact with dogma. This problem of knowledge, evidence, and fact is driving a dangerous turn toward not just decontextualized numbers and a frenzy of empty displays of efficacy for grounding assertions, but worse yet, essentialist identitarian forms of politics that seek to ground truth in allegedly good and bad human bodies. Such essentialist identity politics defines the essence, selfhood, consciousness, and ideological views of members of groups of people by common physical traits. That is, such views falsely comprehend the body as a guarantee of the truth of personhood and perspective. As I explain later in this chapter, the crisis of truth, fact, evidence, and theory is profoundly wrapped up with the recent resurgence of right-wing identity politics committed to white supremacy, anti-Semitism, xenophobia, and sexism as well as rampant conspiracy and political authoritarianism. As Zygmunt Bauman contends, material precarity produced through growing inequality and the upward amassing of wealth drives people to seek security in the Strongman.[2] My argument here is that the estrangement of fact compels a similar frenzied pursuit of security in the false promise of material grounding to be found in numbers and bodies.

The neoliberal restructuring of public education and its revival of positivism is historically implicated in the current crisis of truth, fact, and politics. In addition, the crisis of truth and the alienation of fact must be addressed in part through critical pedagogical projects that reject the culture of positivism and its antitheoretical tendencies and instead can foster critical consciousness, reflective action, and democratic identifications.

THE PERSISTENCE OF POSITIVISM IN EDUCATION

The practices of K–12 schooling and the field of education have a long history with radical empiricism. Empiricist theories of learning date back to John Locke and Jean-Jacques Rousseau with a conception of the student as an empty vessel needing to be filled with knowledge or a blank slate on which to be written. While Auguste Comte conceived of positivism in the nineteenth century, it was not until the early twentieth century that positivist models of teaching and learning were developed from the ideals of industrial efficiency and Frederick Taylor's scientific management.[3] The school was reconceptualized as a factory. Across the United States, the Gary Plan was implemented, in which the time and space of school were organized to model a factory with shifts and bells. Knowledge was imagined as an industrial product that needed to be ever more efficiently produced and transmitted and be consumed by the student. In this view, teachers' work ought to be seen like factory work and could be broken down and made more efficient, speeded up, and measured. From the 1930s to the 1960s, scientific management surged in education. It was bolstered by the rise of educational psychology and its eugenic legacy that sought to establish an empirical science of intelligence, learning, and ability.[4] The eugenics legacy of testing and standardization of knowledge and the learning process merged with the industrial manufacturing promotion of standardization of knowledge as product and process needing to be made ever more efficient. Of course, schooling is a site not just of domination but also resistance to domination and struggle by oppressed classes and cultural groups for social, political, and cultural power. It also represents a struggle over the uses and purposes of public goods and resources.[5]

By the 1970s and 1980s, a growing body of liberal and radical educational scholarship pushed back against radical empiricism. This literature drew on the earlier progressive and radical educational theory of John Dewey and George Counts. Social and Cultural Reproduction theorists and proponents of critical pedagogy also appropriated from Karl Marx, Antonio Gramsci, the Frankfurt School of Critical Theory, and critical sociology as well as from feminist theory, pragmatism, Black studies, and poststructuralism. Unlike the dominant positivist discourses, radical education theory emphasized the inherently political nature of teaching and learning, the politics of knowledge and curriculum, and the assumption that all educational practices are undergirded by theories whether recognized or not. Against the assumption of a universally valuable and disinterested view of schooling, radical educational theorists drew on Gramsci to emphasize the extent to which the school and the curriculum are sites and stakes of class and cultural struggle. Against the positivist view of the subject as a receptacle for commodified units of knowledge, radical education theory, such as that of Paulo Freire and Henry Giroux, emphasized that theory always underpins educational practices and that the question is really whether teachers are aware of the theories that they employ.[6] Radical educators pushed back against the tendency of psychological and developmental radical empiricist approaches to biologize, naturalize, and individualize educational practices. Instead, they emphasized the social, political, and cultural aspects of pedagogy and curriculum.

While critical educational studies drew on a broad array of critical theories in the social sciences and the humanities, most subdisciplines in education in the latter half of the twentieth century were predominantly influenced by empirical psychology. By the late 1990s, economics became the dominant trope through which educational studies were framed. Economic framings of educational problems and solutions from the early 1980s to the present is in no small part due to the expansion

of neoliberal ideology in education and the related accountability movement.

From the 1980s to the present, radical empiricism has played
a central role in the radical restructuring of public education
by bringing together two key trends: (1) neoliberal privatization in its various forms paired and (2) the radically empiricist
accountability and standards movement. Neoliberal privatization involves public sector defunding, privatizations like
charters and vouchers, commercialism, managerialism, and
the ideology of corporate culture. The accountability and standards movement involves extensive standardized testing, high
stakes testing in which funding depends on raised test scores,
standardization of curriculum, and the expansion of technologies for tracking, testing, and homogenizing. Privatization and
accountability are two mutually reinforcing trends with radical empiricism at their centers. Neoliberal privatization has
been justified since the early 1980s by incessant declarations
of the failure of public education. Such declared failure has
been framed through the register of market and military competition, but it has drawn most heavily on selective claims
of numerical standardized test score failures. Test based failures have been claimed through reference to international
and domestic comparisons, such as the Organisation for Economic Co-operation and Development's (OECD) Programme
for International Student Assessment (PISA), Trends in International Mathematics and Science Study (TIMSS), and Progress
in International Reading Literacy Study (PIRLS) scores as well
as to the low test scores of urban schools.[7] Public school failure declarations erase how the tests represent the social class
position of students, their cultural capital, and the radically
different histories of investment in schools and communities. Schools serving the working class and the poor that were
deemed "failed" in part through reference to the test scores
were deemed ripe for experimentation, especially for market intervention. Hence, urban and rural poor schools were

targeted for privatization in the form of chartering, vouchers, for-profit contracting, and corporate managerial reforms.

The accountability and standards movement has itself been a massive for-profit industry in test, textbook, and electronic curricular products. The standardization of curriculum has been promoted as allowing greater control over the delivery and consumption of knowledge. Standardized testing and prescriptive standardized curriculum products have come to dominate the public-school curriculum. Standardized tests erase the process of knowledge making by disappearing the people who make the tests as well as their social positions, interests, and ideological commitments. In this view, facts come from nowhere, are delivered, and are either properly or improperly consumed. Standardized tests evacuate the necessary act of interpretation of fact that is foreclosed by the prescribed choices of four or five possible answers. Such practices make learning seem mechanical, as though one collects little pieces of knowledge along a path that has been established before one encounters it.

Venture philanthropists such as Bill Gates and Eli Broad have spent millions to promote educational administration and leadership that are "data-driven." They have funded database tracking projects that aim to align numerical measures of test performance to behaviors and then use the data to inform and control the behavior of teachers. More recently, philanthrocapitalist entities such as the Chan Zuckerberg Initiative (CZI) and major technology companies are promoting the replacement of teachers and dialogic forms of learning with mass-produced corporate knowledge products that can be quantified and standardized. In this case, the disregard for the specificities of subjectivity and context are sold as their opposite: "personalized learning."[8] As I discuss in my book *Scripted Bodies*, there are radically empiricist projects that now pair positivism with the use of various technologies that chemically control children. For example, nootropic drugs or smart drugs, typically amphetamines, are used to drug kids to make them pay attention when taking standardized tests or to control themselves so that they do not disturb other kids' testing. Grit pedagogy revives behaviorism through tactics for learned bodily self-control—a new corporeally targeted education for developing neoliberal character. In the tradition of positivism, the dominant educational reforms presume that knowledge and learning are delinked from both the experience of the student and from the broader social world.

So, on one hand, educational policy and practice have become thoroughly dominated by the assumption that what matters most is just the facts. On the other hand, there is an incredible disregard for facts, information, evidence, or reasoned argument when it comes to the most dominant educational policy pushes. For example, Donald Trump's Secretary of Education Betsy DeVos spent 20 years promoting educational privatization in Michigan. DeVos promoted for-profit chartering and vouchers. Both policies have an empirical record of poor performance in test-based achievement.[9] However, there is a long legacy of right-wing promotion of failed market-based reform. There is an extensive empirical record of the disaster of vouchers internationally—a record of gutting the public education system, of vastly exacerbating unequal quality schools, and causing the proliferation of cheap, bad, for-profit schools for the poor.[10] Vouchers in the U.S. have long been promoted as a way to get a foot in the door for educational privatization. Once a single market-based scheme can be launched, then right wing think tanks can call for more studies, more experiments. During the COVID-19 pandemic, right-wing think tanks advocated the expansion of vouchers and neo-voucher scholarship tax credits to have the public pay for privatization and deregulation of schools in the form of "microschools" or pods, especially for-profit ones. They do so even as no evidence exists to support these schemes, even as the think tanks admit that they are racially and class exclusionary, and even as the voucher and neovoucher schemes have been established as worsening racial segregation and educational resource inequality.[11] The market and the erosion of the public schools in this discourse is its own justification.

Another clear case in point of a complete disregard for evidence is the right-wing promotion of charter schooling as a catalyst to replace public schooling with a private industry. Andy Smarick in the Hoover Institution's magazine *Education Next* was quite explicit that the right should champion charters in the short run to justify declaration of charters as a failed public experiment and to justify more widespread privatization.[12] Paul T. Hill, like Smarick, calls for "churn" or "creative destruction." Hill, of the neoliberal Center for Reinventing Public Education, relentlessly promoted "urban portfolio districts" in order to expand charter-based privatization and admitted in his advocacy work that there would be no way to empirically ascertain whether or not the urban portfolio model of "churn," opening and closing schools and chartering, would result in improvements of academic performance.[13] However, Hill insisted that the privatizations afforded by the model justify it. Smarick, Hill, and other market fundamentalists aim to replace public education with a private for-profit industry in education.

The thinking of such ideologues was behind the radical privatization of public education in New Orleans after hurricane Katrina and in Chicago following the razing of its public housing projects. After the storm, the New Orleans public schools and the teacher's union was dismantled and replaced by a network of four charter districts. Chicago closed a significant portion of its neighborhood public schools and replaced them with charters. Recently, scholars such as Sean Reardon at Stanford and journalists such as David Leonhardt of *the New York Times* have promoted claims that New Orleans and Chicago represent evidence of school improvement following radical neoliberal restructuring (school closures, privatizations, and union busting), pointing to small increases in standardized test scores.[14] But by 2017, New Orleans saw a 3-year decline in test scores, and most studies of Chicago charters find nearly identical test scores as for neighborhood schools. Meanwhile, those making these claims of improvement are studiously ignoring the massive displacement of working class and poor students and families from these sections of cities combined with rising family incomes from gentrification. Standardized tests consistently correlate with family income.[15] Following Katrina in New Orleans, the poorest families were dispossessed of their communities. The new four charter districts represent a different population than the one prior to the storm. Similarly, following the massive planned gentrification/public housing and neighborhood school closures coordinated by the Commercial Club of Chicago and more than a decade of steadily rising family incomes in the city, the tests are measuring different students, and most importantly, richer students. As sociologist Pierre Bourdieu explained, the reason that test scores correlate to family income is because the tests measure the knowledge, tastes, and dispositions of professional and ruling class people who also happen to be the ones who commission and make the tests.[16] So, we have a situation where rich investors are pushing the poorest people out of cities, putting in place market-based school reforms, testing the new population, and claiming that the reforms rather than the dispossession caused the alleged improvements. These empirical studies not only misrepresent positivist standardized tests as definitive evidence of meaningful learning, but they also fail to account for epidemic cases of charters pushing out the students who are the hardest to educate, including those requiring special education, English language learners, and those identified as discipline problems. These claims of neoliberal restructuring success are examples of ideological uses of evidence for justifying a privatization agenda.

Mark Fisher described in his book *Capitalist Realism* this fictive performance of quantifiable efficacy as "market Stalinism."[17]

The contradiction between the imperative for radical empiricist approaches to policy and practice and the abandonment of evidence and argumentation is playing out in media culture and more specifically, news and journalism.

WHAT ANTITHEORY HAS TO DO WITH FAKE NEWS, BAD JOURNALISM, AND CONSPIRACY

Following the election of Donald Trump, numerous essays in the popular press offered explanations for how a flagrant and compulsive liar with no regard for truth or evidence could garner widespread support. A lot of politicians lie, but the quantity and brazenness of Trump's lies represented a broader disregard for empirical evidence and for education. Over the course of Trump's tenure in office, he publicly lied or made misleading statements 30,573 times.[18] Examples of the disregard for evidence range from insisting that Obama was not born in the United States to a rejection of the scientific consensus about human-caused climate change, to scapegoating undocumented immigrants by accusing them of rape and murder, to the making of impossible claims about financing a border wall, to describing his loss of the popular vote as winning by a landslide, to nominating such figures as Mike Flynn to head the US National Security Agency (Flynn falsely claims that Sharia (Islamic law) is being built in the United States, and his reputation for untruth got his statements in the military derided as "Flynn Facts"). Examples of Trump's disregard for education include stating that he "likes the uneducated," to appointing Education Secretary Betsy DeVos, who throughout her tenure remained committed to expanding vouchers and for-profit charter schooling, even though her efforts in Michigan resulted in overwhelming empirical evidence that these policies worsen schools and lower test scores.[19] DeVos also financially supported organizations dedicated to expanding the use of public money for private religious education, and she used public money to bail out failing for-profit colleges that committed fraud. DeVos's actions raised questions as to her commitment to truth, fact, and evidence, as did her investments in a sham brain treatment center called "Neurocore" that shows movies to children with autism and ADHD and interrupts them when they stop paying attention.[20] After investigations revealed the lack of evidence for the pseudoscientific "brain training techniques" and revealed DeVos's refusal to file ethics and recusal statements for possible conflicts of interest, DeVos and her husband significantly expanded their multimillion dollar investments in the company.[21]

Popular press explanations for the acceptability and even widespread embrace of un-truth include varieties of "blame the internet." One version of blame the internet offers the "fake news" narrative, in which the abundance of ersatz news stories rendered the population incapable of distinguishing real from fake news. The stories about fake news imply that "real news" could allow citizens to make informed choices. But such "real news" covered the 2016 election with nearly no investigative journalism or dissection of the untruths spoken by politicians, and with minimal analysis of policy proposals. However, "real news" suffers from saturation by commercial promotional content.

Media theorist Robert McChesney has demonstrated that the decline of investigative journalism must be understood as the result of corporate media consolidation rather than internet competition for news outlets.[22] The decline of investigative journalism has resulted in news consisting of about 90 percent public relations content. As corporate media venues covered fake news and its role in the election, right-wing media outlets propelled by Trump's claims began characterizing mainstream media news itself as fake news. Outlandish fake news stories were generated in part to drive internet clickthrough profits, especially during the 2016 presidential election. Web entrepreneurs wrote sensational stories, such as one about Hillary Clinton operating a pedophile prostitution ring out of a pizza parlor: "Pizzagate." An armed vigilante intent on saving the victims fired his rifle in the restaurant only to discover that Hillary Clinton and the children she was pimping were not there. Of course, Pizzagate is but one sensational example among the vast growth of fake news from QAnon and replacement conspiracies to antivaccination movements and the more quotidian corporate public relations stories designed to sell things or influence politics (e.g., undermining environmentalism).

The problem of the news media involves not only the extent to which content production has been compromised by commerce but also the extent to which educative institutions have failed to provide citizens with the tools needed to interpret the quality of sources and veracity of claims. For example, most Americans have not learned about the standards and varieties of editorial review, such as journalistic and scholarly review, and the differences between these and an internet posting. Functional literacy now requires the capacity to distinguish sources of information, lest we all heroically invade pedophile prostitution pizza parlors. But functional literacy is not enough.

One crucial element missing from the discussion of fake news is the way that both professional journalism and fake news disavow the politics of knowledge behind claims to truth. Mainstream journalism effaces its own framing assumptions and theoretical presuppositions behind the framing of narratives, the collection of facts, and the interpretation of the meaning of those facts. Rightist critics of media began describing mainstream journalism as fake news, alleging that mainstream journalism is a collection of false facts, rather than criticizing the underlying values, assumptions, and positions that underlie the narratives. Following allegations that fake news was involved in Trump's election, Trump himself declared CNN "fake news," and he repeated and expanded this accusation.

Trump got this right but for the wrong reasons. Most of the time, the problem with CNN is not ludicrous made-up stories but the failure to examine competing values, assumptions, and ideologies behind claims to truth as well as the relationship between these symbolic contests and material ones. The lie built into mainstream media is the guise of disinterested objectivity, in which ruling class and dominant cultural group interests are universalized, or as the *New York Times* motto puts it, as "All the News That's Fit to Print." Corporate media juxtaposes falsehoods in the fake news with its own allegedly disinterested and neutral "true" news coverage. The missing element from both perspectives is consideration of the theory behind the organization of and interpretation of fact. The lie of disinterested objectivity is the same lie that is built into standardized tests and curricula.

News media could draw on an endless pool of scholarly experts who would analyze and theorize about current events at no cost. Instead, the prevalence of vapid news media punditry and yelling heads making unbacked assertions, in place of investigative journalism or scholarly analysis, has both financial and ideological dimensions. Advertising drives content. Amplifying volume and spectacle delivers emotionally stimulated viewers to ads. Keeping scholarly experts off news programming avoids the introduction of ideologically dangerous questions about power, politics, and history that might raise doubts about ruling class and ruling cultural group priorities.

Another popular press explanation for the crisis of truth has to do with the alleged nature of the Trump supporters. Writing in *The Nation* magazine, Susan McWilliams provides the "Hunter Thompson Hell's Angel's Revenge Theory" of the angry white working-class male.[23] In this explanation for the affirmation of untruth by the electorate, decades of alienation driven by neoliberal globalization have resulted in an economically and politically excluded population of white men who are driven primarily by revenge on political and educated elites. In this narrative, Trump's rejection of fact, evidence, and truth is not a problem for supporters, because they are well aware that politics is a show and, most importantly, believed that Donald Trump the showman would stick it to elites (of course, after the election, he proceeded to stock the government with Wall Street and billionaire elites, who have aggressively redistributed wealth upward while targeting the caregiving social state). This perspective suggests that the real promise of Trump was one of subverting the elite establishment. In fact, the more transgressive Trump's statements became, the more credence they gave to the perception that he was a true threat to the ruling establishment and was not beholden to the rules of a game that elites had rigged against most of the population. Hence, Trump provided a point of identification for citizens in which his lies were a catalyst to a greater truth that the mainstream media, political class, academics, and economic elites largely didn't want to admit— that an ostensibly fair system is in fact a system rigged by and for elites at the expense of most. Like critical theorists, the Trump voter is deeply suspicious of appearances. However, the critical theorist wants to take experience, appearance, and claims to truth on a detour through theory.

Theory provides an examination of the values, assumptions, and ideologies that undergird claims to truth. It allows facts to be interpreted and situated in terms of broader structural and systemic patterns, history, and context. Theory also allows one to comprehend how the interpretive scaffold of the subject is formed by the social and how the social is formed of subjects. Theory allows one to reflect on one's actions, and it expands the language to mediate experience and interpret facts. As Adorno states, "only speculation which can penetrate external reality, and show what really and truly lies behind the façade of facticity that is asserting itself, can be said to do justice to reality. . . . The only way to capture reality and the true experience of it is to go beyond the immediate givens of experience."[24] Theory expands political agency, and political agency is crucial for a democratic society.

The Trumpian voter employs conspiracy rather than theory. Conspiracy imagines that there are superagents endowed with the ability to secretly determine outcomes. In the logic of conspiracy, those on the outside of the conspiracy are left with spectatorial agency—able to get a glimpse of the conspiracy but without the tools to make sense of what produced a particular social phenomenon or experience. Bad superagents, the conspirators, conspire to conceal fact, propagate lies, and shape history in the shadows. Only good superagents (such as a charismatic and strong leader), who allegedly embody truth, can reveal the conspiracy (that is, fabricate it) and then shape history on behalf of the victims of the conspirators. In contrast, the conspirators do not simply speak untruth; they embody untruth. The problem for the Nazis wasn't that the Jews believed the wrong thing and needed to be reeducated to the right views. It was who they were: their essence, their nature. The problem for Trump and the alt-right is not radical Islam but Muslims themselves. Hence, the ban on travel from Muslim majority countries under the pretext of security, even though there had been no terrorist attacks by individuals of those nations since before September 11. For conspiracy, the identity-based grounding of the enemy is not a coincidence but rather is consistent with the need for a material grounding to anchor the accusation. The body of the scapegoated functions like numbers in the world of alienated fact, providing an aura of foundation for scapegoating and lies. As I detail in later chapters, this is perhaps nowhere more evident than in the replacement conspiracy theories (chanted in Charlottesville "Jews will not replace us" and motivating the Tree of Life Synagogue shooting) in which Jews, Muslims, immigrants, Blacks, women, homosexuals, and other minorities are alleged to be replacing straight White Christian men or acting as secret agents to replace them.

From vaccines causing autism to fluoride in drinking water, birtherism, chemtrails to 9/11 conspiracy, Holocaust denial, QAnon, and so on, a frenzy of irrationalism belies a deep distrust of facts and yet a faith in fact unmoored from the history and context that gives fact its meaning. In a culture in which positivism suggests the supremacy of the fact, fact is decontextualized and dehistoricized, appearing to come from nowhere—to be all powerful and yet deeply suspicious. In *History and Freedom,* Adorno states that "the world of facts has degenerated into a cloak, a veil that conceals what is essentially real." [25] Some of what is "essentially real" for Adorno that is obscured by the positivist fetishism for immediacy and the swindle of concreteness are "the laws of motion of society, especially the laws which express how the present situation has come into being and where it is tending to go." [26] The false promise of concreteness in facts denies such essentials as: a society structured around class antagonism; the capitalist exchange principle; the enlightenment logic of the domination and mastery of nature; the self, structured through the social antagonisms of the larger society; and the possibility of mediation and critique, negating the world as it is and imagining a different future in part by the practice of theorizing.

In such a context of decontextualized fact, the repetition of baseless assertions and lies flourishes. The positivist legacy provides enabling cultural conditions for authoritarians who are hostile to democratic cultures of free exchange of knowledge, the value of which is established by superior argument and evidence. Positivism supports those who prefer knowledge to be grounded by the social authority of the claimant, locating the concept in the subject rather than in society. It supports affirmation of existing oppressive structures and systems in part through a misrepresentation of social reality as static rather than dynamic.[27]

Another popular explanation for the embrace of untruth could be called the "mainstreaming of postmodernism" position. This view suggests that we are now living in a "post-truth" era, in which most people recognize that uncertainties about facts, spin, or partial narratives are the new norm. Such a view can be seen in popular discourse when George W. Bush's chief of staff Karl Rove derided journalists in the "reality-based community" who criticized the president for ignoring reality. Rove claimed that, by acting, those in power make a new reality. Stephen Colbert named the tendency to ignore facts when making assertions "truthiness." Oil and tobacco companies have long embraced postmodern truth by hiding their own empirical studies of lung cancer and human-caused climate change. They insist that there are a multitude of competing narratives and bodies of evidence, and hence, these dangers cannot be grounded. In the absence of definitive proof, let's keep burning fossil fuels and cigarettes. Critics of this mainstreaming of postmodern truth view refer to the material limits of epistemological uncertainty. Facts matter like the fact of gravity when jumping out of a window. However, Trump's and the Republican party's open and irrational rejection of empirical evidence is very different from antifoundationalism in its pragmatist, postmodern, or critical theory forms, in which competing narratives, arguments, and evidence call into question the possibility of access to certain knowledge of objective reality. As in science, these positions share a comfort with truth being provisional, antifoundational, and fallible: The best theoretical assumptions, arguments, and evidence win until better ones can displace them.

FROM THE ALIENATION OF FACT TO CRITICAL PEDAGOGY

How do we make sense of this glaring contradiction between, on one hand, the imperative for positivism in which the fact is positioned as the supreme self-evident value, and, on the other hand, the abandonment of fact, evidence, or even truth itself when it comes to speech and policy? What explains these contradictions playing out in both educational and media discourse is (1) the alienation of fact and (2) the related replacement of reasoned argument with faith/dogma.

Critical theory has a long tradition of analyzing how dogma sediments in social consciousness. Theodor Adorno, for example, offered an explanation for the allure of positivism. Adorno explained that in a capitalist world in which everything is for sale, everything loses its value other than as a means of abstract exchange. While Marx described the alienation, abstraction, and emptying out of social relations in capitalism, Adorno explains the promise of numbers as a false promise of concreteness and immediacy that responds to the tendency for abstraction.[28] This loss of value renders all things abstract, and everything in the social world is experienced as floating and ephemeral. Numbers promise to restore the solidity and certainty of concreteness and immediacy lost through alienation. We can think about this promise with respect to standardized testing. Standardized testing has now been dominating public education for nearly 20 years, since No Child Left Behind was launched in 2001. Knowledge is decontextualized and truth claims are delinked from their conditions of production in the standardized test. Yet the attachment of numbers to test performance provides a scientistic aura of certainty that recontextualizes knowledge and the test taker within a system of educational exchange that leads through academic promotion to a promise ultimately of economic exchange. The attachment of numbers to truth claims and their false promise of certainty and solidity has resulted in a now-dominant way of thinking about learning as earning. It has transformed a generations' way of thinking about learning as instrumental and grade motivated, equated knowledge with authority, and evacuated curiosity that is not contextualized through numerical reward.

Numerical quantification applies not science but a guise of science or scientism, invoking a careful and systematic process of measurement.[29] It also suggests disinterestedness, objectivity, and universality. It provides a feeling of control by invoking abstract objectivity and universality. Although numbering things offers a response to the alienation of market exchange everywhere, it is also alienating in its tendency to delimit the relationship between subjectivity and the objective world.

To extend Adorno's insight, we might consider those activities to which the attachment of numerical quantification is anathema. Numbers do not promise certainty and solidity in certain contexts. Think about your closest relationships, the people you care most about. Imagine those you love providing a numerical rating for your affections. "Dinner with you was an 8.5." Imagine telling a joke with a friend and getting a numerical rating in return. What these examples highlight is that our pleasures for human intimacy and intersubjective connection are contrary to the promise of numerical control offered by positivism. Quantification as a remedy for alienation simultaneously offers a guise of control while creating more alienation. Those suffering from OCD often have a need to apply numerical rituals to experiences. For example, to leave a room, someone with OCD may need to open and close the door a certain number of times or count the number of steps to the door. The counting provides a temporary feeling of control otherwise experienced as lacking in these individuals. The numbers do not fix the obsession; they just briefly sooth the anxiety. Is not the ideology of positivism a kind of collective OCD that offers a soothing yet false promise of control over a physical world experienced as slipping away, melting into air? The alienation of fact involves the disappearance of the conditions of production of fact, the mystification of fact, and the treatment of fact as dogma to be transmitted and received.

What stands behind the absence of evidence and reasoned argument in educational policy and practice is faith—a faith in markets. The faith in markets is not only the result of decades of neoliberal ideology and the promotion of the TINA thesis

(There Is No Alternative—to the market) but also of decades of schooling in which knowledge has been positioned as true by virtue of the authority of the claimant. The era of standardized testing has effectively accomplished this equation of truth with authority by alienating truth claims, making them appear to come from nowhere and having authority by virtue of their anonymous authorship. Standardized tests do not come with the tools to question or dispute; they defy dialogue and follow the logic of monologue.

In my book, *The Failure of Corporate School Reform,* I discuss the relationship between the new uses of positivism in education and market fundamentalism or capitalist dogma. What I term the "new market positivism" is typified by the reinvigorated expansion of longstanding positivist approaches to schooling: standardized testing, standardization of curriculum, the demand for policy grounded exclusively in allegedly scientific (really scientistic) empirically based pedagogical reforms, and the drumbeat against educational theory and in favor of practicalism. The new market positivism signals the use of these longstanding approaches toward the expansion of multiple forms of educational privatization.

In the Fordist era, positivism neutralized, naturalized, and universalized social and cultural reproduction under the guise of the public good, the public interest, but also individual values of humanist education. Critical educational scholars of the 1970s and 1980s referred to this obscuring of the capitalist reproduction function of the public school as "the hidden curriculum." The economic role of schooling as a sorting and sifting mechanism for the capitalist economy was largely denied. As Pierre Bourdieu and Jean Passeron pointed out, such mechanisms as tests and grades simultaneously stratify based on class while concealing how merit and talent stand in for the unequal distribution of life chances.[30] Reproduction in the new market positivism still neutralizes and naturalizes the unequal distribution of life chances through the unequal distribution of cultural and social capital. Class mobility in the United States is far less possible today than in the past. But the new market positivism also openly naturalizes and universalizes a particular economic basis for all educational relationships while justifying a shift in governance and control over educational institutions. Positivist testing and database projects that purport to be efficient knowledge delivery systems and that reward or punish teachers are not only at the center of pedagogical, curricular, and administrative reform, but they are also openly justified through the allegedly universal benefits of capitalism. The new market positivism subjects all to standardization and normalization of knowledge, denying class and cultural interests and the political struggle behind the organization and framing of claims to truth. The new market positivism links its denial and concealment of the politics of knowledge to its open and aggressive application of capitalist ideology—that is, the faith in the religion of capitalism—to every aspect of public schooling.

In *Escape from Freedom*, Erich Fromm suggests that the very possibility of modern rationality comes from disobedience, dislocation, and estrangement.[31] The child's "no" introduces a separation from parental authority. For Fromm, the social and historical conditions for self-reflection come from the alienating effects of capitalism. Only by being estranged from the land and labor and social relations can one make an object of analysis of oneself and society. Paulo Freire, Henry Giroux, and others followed Fromm's thought in advocating the making of both subjective experience and analysis of the objective social world objects of critical analysis. In the tradition of critical pedagogy, the process of theorizing self and society creates the conditions for humanization and agency by countering capitalist objectification in its many forms.

As both liberals and conservatives continue to embrace positivist forms of education and journalism, they contribute to the alienation of fact and the crisis of truth that it creates.

Against the "bad alienation of fact" of radical empiricism that decontextualizes and dehistoricizes truth claims, critical pedagogy puts forward what we could call a "good alienation of fact" that seeks to contextualize and comprehend not only the theoretical assumptions and ideological underpinnings but also the broader material interests, social forces, and symbolic contests that are imbricated with claims to truth. Critical pedagogy estranges experience and truth claims by denaturalizing them and treating them as an object of analysis. Critical pedagogy reinvests claims to truth with the conditions of their production—that is, the history, context, and social contests that give meaning to truth claims. It provides an approach to knowledge that emphasizes how acts of interpretation of fact can form the basis for social intervention. Critical pedagogy fosters democratic dispositions, including linking the process of learning to engagement with public problems and the commitment to dialogic forms of learning and public life. As such, critical pedagogy asserts the potential for fact, when theorized and interpreted, to be a source of agency rather than an oppressive alienated force.

2 ARTIFICIAL INTELLIGENCE AND DIGITAL EDUCATIONAL PRIVATIZATION

Contemporary concerns about the potentially nefarious tendencies of artificial intelligence (AI) technology have become widespread in public and popular cultural discourse. These range from anxiety about AI coming to consciousness, usurping human control over other machines and infrastructure, and annihilating humanity (as in the movies *Terminator, Ex Machina,* and Elon Musk's many apocalyptic warnings), to AI's uses in automating inequality[1] in public service agencies to conceal austerity agendas that target the poor, to concerns about surveillance capitalism[2] that eradicates privacy while translating human experience into behavioral data that forms the basis for prediction products and behavioral futures markets. While many of these fears are warranted, a great deal of the fear of AI applications depends on a false assumption that the technology has a kind of mystical transcendent agency that evades human capacities for governing it. Instead, the ways that the technology is being implemented in education illustrate longstanding economic, political, and ideological agendas and interests.[3] The positioning of the technology as an autonomous force delinked from human control conceals the material and symbolic interests served by the technology. Thus, the strategic erasure of human agency obscures the very targeted uses of the tech. What is more, as I discuss below, the misrepresentation of data as delinked from culture and politics, as allegedly disinterested and neutral, obscures the inevitable political and ethical norms and values that particular education projects (including AI education) animate and enact.

This chapter argues that the development of for-profit AI technologies largely fosters the privatization of public education and concomitant erosion of the values, practices, and critical forms of democratic education. In what follows, I situate the advent of digital technologies in the context of structural economic and ideological shifts of the past 40 years. Such changes include neoliberal restructuring, the repressive turn in schools and society, changes in the use of positivist ideology in schooling, the role of new technologies in social and cultural reproduction and changing imperatives for capital accumulation. Sections of the chapter illustrate different uses of AI as part of the technological transformation of the privatization of public education and consider AI in relation to the broader structural and ideological context. I consider the ways that AI continues longstanding trends through the promotion of adaptive learning technology and transformations to teacher work and conceptions of knowledge and learning; biometric pedagogy and the cultural politics of locating learning in the body; and the convergence of impact investing and digital surveillance technologies. Changes in the ownership and control over different aspects of public schooling relate to the cultural politics of knowledge and learning.

I first review three significant AI applications in education: adaptive learning technology, biometric pedagogy, and the intersection of Social Impact Bonds/pay for success with digital surveillance. The sections that follow take up these AI education examples in relation to the longer-standing legacies of neoliberal privatization, repression, and positivism for social and cultural reproduction. The sections consider how the uses of AI continue and how they break with prior trends and tendencies. The chapter concludes by considering how and what place there might be for the values of democratic education in the uses of these new technologies. By illustrating the democratic possibilities of an AI education project, at the end of the chapter, I emphasize that the social and ethical implications of the technology itself are not fixed or determined.

AI EDUCATION

According to the 2016 White House report, "Preparing for the Future of Artificial Intelligence," "a core objective of AI research and applications over the years has been to automate or replicate intelligent behavior."[4] In education, numerous companies pursue narrow AI rather than general AI that aspires to automating general intelligence and machine autonomy. Narrow AI, which attempts to outperform humans at a particular task, "underpins many commercial services such as trip planning, shopper recommendation systems, and ad targeting, and is finding important applications in medical diagnosis, education, and scientific research."[5] Williamson, Pykett, and Nemorin detail some AI projects that are under way. The authors analyze tests, textbook and media giant Pearson's AI projects including "data analytics techniques, machine learning algorithms, computer modelling, statistics, artificial neural networks and neuroscience."[6] Some of the most significant AI projects involve for-profit educational endeavors that push profit-seeking into schooling in relatively new ways.

For-profit AI education companies and for-profit education businesses are coming together. As I have argued elsewhere,[7] corporate media is converging with corporate education sectors as large media corporations (such as Apple, Microsoft, Facebook/Chan Zuckerberg Initiative (CZI), and Alphabet/Google) have become major for-profit education companies, and traditional educational test and textbook purveyors (such as Pearson NCS, Houghton-Mifflin, McGraw-Hill, and Wiley Education) have increasingly become media corporations. In addition, longstanding for-profit educational contractors have moved into AI. For example, Knewton (acquired by Wiley Education in 2019) was spun off from Edison Learning, one of the largest for-profit educational management organizations. Collectively, such for-profit corporations have shifted ownership, design, and control of curriculum and pedagogical practice from teachers to business. Bolstering a neoliberal ideology that positions public education as a business and in the service of business, ideologies of techno-utopian progress, technological disruptions, and the equating of technology with economic growth have played a large part in the exponential growth of digital technology in schools.[8]

Despite the prevalence of techno-utopian ideology, some of the actual applications have ranged from the questionable and ineffectual to the outright embarrassing. For example, in Los Angeles, billions of dollars were spent on tablets that could not be used, and young children were found to be drawing on them with crayons. No empirical evidence exists to support the success of AI applications of adaptive learning technology in traditional measures of test-based achievement.[9] Beyond the ways that unproven technology displaces sound educational practice, the usurpation of pedagogy and curriculum has significant implications for how people understand the relationships between learning and the self, knowledge and social context, and the roles and purposes of schools. Techno-utopianism is thoroughly wrapped up with what has become the dominant justification for schooling—the means for youth to become workers and consumers and the means for nations to compete in the global economy. Learning as the means of social and political agency and democratic self-governance has been crowded out of the education technology discourse. Indeed, at the time when, according to tech leaders Zuckerberg, Musk, and Gates, the futures of capitalism, the environment, and work itself are increasingly called into question by technological development (more specifically, AI), the ideologies of technological utopianism and determinism are ubiquitous in public and policy discourse.[10]

Some of the most prevalent for-profit endeavors of AI in education involve producing student data that is then sold, contracting with public entities to get for-profit technologies into schools, and making the management and influence of behavior and the body into data products.[11] In addition, these initiatives collapse the distinction between for-profit private industries and nonprofit public entities. Three such projects are adaptive learning technology, biometric pedagogy technology, and the quantification of impact investing schemes through machine learning. These three projects exemplify the ways that AI in education allows for expanded privatization, contracting, and labor expropriation while undermining the democratic culture and possibilities of schooling as a means for the broader democratization of society. I summarize the technologies here first and then discuss them together in terms of the key concerns with economic exploitation, the de-democratization of schooling, and the legacies of prior forms of educational privatization.

Adaptive Learning Technology

CZI's adaptive learning technology platform Summit exemplifies the varieties of profit seeking in technology. While Summit offers school districts its basic program for free, the fuller implementation requires payment. Summit is part of a limited liability company (LLC), CZI, that includes such for-profit pay-for-fee educational services as Byju's and other for-profits that were acquired exclusively for capturing user data. The LLC structure makes the movement of money, not to mention data, among these subunits secret and unaccountable to public oversight. Summit was developed by Facebook engineers, and although Summit does not have advertisements, it is, like Facebook, a data production engine. A major concern of adaptive learning technology in education involves the ways it appropriates private data about youth: "Like Summit, Canvas connects children to third-party sites (such as YouTube) that collects data for advertising purposes, and it denies responsibility for any use a third party might make of children's or teachers' data. Companies may share aggregated and de-identified data without notice to users, despite evidence that such de-identified data is easily re-identified."[12]

Roberts-Mahony, Means, and Garrison (2016) liken adaptive learning to the "netflixing" of education. Purporting to be "personalized," adaptive learning technology tailors content or the pace of delivery to students. Proponents of adaptive learning technology claim that their products individualize instruction and are attentive to individual needs, pace, and capacity, and so they overcome pedagogical standardization, homogenized curriculum, and excessive testing. Mainstream criticism of adaptive learning technology points out that evidence does not exist for its efficacy as measured by standardized test scores,[13] and that it represents a form of privatization and commercialism by shifting control over curriculum and pedagogy from teachers and schools to for-profit corporations.

As I have shown elsewhere,[14] under the rubric of "personalization," adaptive learning programs undermine genuine personalization by delinking knowledge and learning from the subjectivities, differences, and experiences of students and their cultures and communities. These programs also prevent students from comprehending themselves as socially formed and from comprehending knowledge as a source of social and political agency. For example, CZI's Summit Learning platform employs a traditional curriculum organized around the Common Core State Standards.[15] The mostly online pedagogy aims to deliver this curriculum. Despite being sold as "personalized," the curriculum does not relate the subjects of study and lessons to students lived experience or the broader social world that informs the interpretation of that experience. About the only things that are "personalized" are that the automated content delivery is accelerated or decelerated based on the student's activity, and the student's use of the software is made into a data case about their progress. The technology platform is positioned as the teacher, the human teacher is sidelined as a "mentor," and constant testing of standardized knowledge and skills are centered, routinized, and converted to metrics. As a result, the teacher is left with little autonomy to make lessons meaningful to students by linking learning to student experience and to make such meaningful learning critical or socially transformative. In fact, the transformation of learning in the use of a canned curriculum entirely delivered on screens has been experienced by large numbers of students and communities as physically taxing (headaches and hand cramps) and devoid of the benefits of personal interaction—it is profoundly alienating.[16] In places as varied as Wellington, Kansas, and Providence, Rhode Island, families and communities rejected the platform.[17]

Adaptive learning technologies create the conditions for student activity to be collected as data and for this collected data to be bought and sold and financialized as investment securities, regardless of whether the student advances. That is, adaptive learning technology stands to revive and deepen longstanding tracking, sorting, and sifting of students based on alleged ability. While proponents of adaptive learning technology claim to reduce testing, the technology and curriculum have been developed around constant testing and teaching to the tests. The tests are misframed as conveying universally valuable, disinterested, and objective knowledge. But the constant testing accomplishes what standardized tests typically do. Namely, the tests obscure the cultural politics of knowledge that informs the selection of knowledge to be taught, and they circumscribe the range of possible interpretations and interpretive frameworks for claims to truth. The tests prohibit an approach to knowledge in which students comprehend claims to truth in relation to material and

symbolic antagonisms, interests, ideologies, and social positions. Adaptive learning technology pushes standardized and
transmission-oriented approaches to teaching that rely on
the promise of technological innovation and the ideology of
corporate culture as a justification. The standardization and
homogenization of knowledge and curriculum and the treatment of knowledge as a consumable commodity both promote
a particular conception of the relationship between knowledge and agency. Knowledge appears as something, made by
others with authority elsewhere, to consume and regurgitate
rather than as something discovered and produced through
dialogic exchange. Knowledge is not presented to students as a
means to interpret experience and the social world so as to act
on and shape that world. The pedagogies of adaptive learning
technology stand in stark contrast with, for example, critical
pedagogies that foster deliberation, debate, dissent, and investigation of the relationships between claims to truth and the
interests, authority, and social positions of those who make
the claims.

The form that adaptive learning platforms tend to take needs
to be comprehended in relation to the structure and interests
of the parent companies. CZI misrepresents itself as a philanthropy when it largely operates as a business. Due to its LLC
corporate structure, CZI muddles for-profit and nonprofit sub-
sidiaries, moves money secretly, refuses public oversight and
accountability, and operates as a for-profit business running
pay-for-fee services, grabbing student data that it commodifies
from its "free services."[18] CZI and other "philanthrocapitalists," such as Emerson Initiative and Omidyar Network, collectively mark a significant shift in philanthropy from the
still-large venture philanthropy mode. Venture philanthropists, such as Gates, Walton, and Broad, founded nonprofit
foundations that promote a neoliberal agenda of educational
privatization and the imposition of corporate managerial
culture in school leadership.[19] Venture philanthropists have

facilitated the usurpation of educational and policy governance over education by superrich individuals and corporations. Philanthrocapitalists erode the distinction between public and private altogether in their organizations, eliding the difference between private interest and public good.

Biometric Pedagogy Technology

As I detailed in *Scripted Bodies*,[20] biometric analytic pedagogy uses AI technology to teach by measuring bodies. Some systems utilize skin-sensing bracelets, and others employ webcam video cameras connected to software platforms that analyze changes to students' bodies in response to a lesson. Based on consumer marketing feedback devices, webcam systems (such as Affdex) measure positive and negative valences and other metrics of attention to the teacher. Biometric pedagogy devices convert physical movements into data and correlate body movements to presumed internal cognitive and emotional reactions that are assumed to be reactions to teacher behavior. This data then becomes the basis for the evaluation of the efficacy of the teacher, the learning of the student. The data is supposed to be able to inform the teacher's pedagogical responses in real time. Machine learning is involved in recognition and comparison of physical movements.

Biometric pedagogy devices presume that learning is the result not of the dialogue-based exchange between teacher and students but rather of the successful impact of the teacher on the student as measured by the student's body. The body as measure of learning and the equation of physical dispositions with learning displaces not only traditional conceptions of learning through dialogic exchange. It also displaces questioning, thinking, and the recognition that students mediate or resist what they learn in sometimes contradictory ways. Although dialogue offers ways for students and teachers to work through those contradictions, biometric pedagogy does not. Biometric pedagogy presumes a direct, transparent, and simplistic notion of learning as depositing of knowledge. What is more, the uses of biometric pedagogy in, for example, the teacher clinical practice assessment system edTPA treats teaching as a scripted performance that aims to elicit a particular physical response from students that may or may not correlate with learning. edTPA is a Pearson product that evaluates student teaching as a recorded performance that is measured by a standardized rubric. The quality and value of teaching can be read off of the body. In this case, biometric pedagogy revives behaviorist and Taylorist approaches to labor aimed at breaking down the tasks and subtasks of workers to make them increasingly approximate a continually raised targeted norm prescribed from the outset. Such prescription fosters an approach to teaching that denies the subjectivities of learners, the particular context for learning, and the broader social structures, systems, and forces that inform the meaning of knowledge and the interpretive acts of teaching and learning.

Quantification of Impact Investing Schemes Through Machine Learning

Pay for Success or Social Impact Bonds are not themselves AI technologies. Pay for Success utilizes digital surveillance technology and has been increasingly merging with AI applications for targeting potential victims/beneficiaries of Social Impact Bond services, pricing of services, automation of services, and risk profiling of students. Aleron social impact consultancy (https://aleronpartners.com) typifies this convergence. Social Impact Bonds are privatization investment schemes that have, since roughly 2010, rapidly expanded in size, scope, and reach of implementation. Social Impact Bonds, which are promoted in the Every Student Succeeds Act (the latest iteration of the Elementary and Secondary Education Act of 1965) bring together banks, philanthropic foundations, and governments in order to privatize public services.[21] Social Impact Bonds partner investment banks, such as Goldman Sachs, with governments (like the city of Chicago or the state of Massachusetts) and are facilitated by nonprofit foundations (like Rockefeller) as well as some universities (like Harvard). Social Impact Bonds identify programs like a juvenile justice recidivism reduction program or an early childhood education program to be funded by the investment bank and to be evaluated for efficacy by an allegedly independent evaluator. The investor pays for the service, and if the metrics suggest the service was a success, then the public repays the investor much more money than it would have cost the public to pay for the service directly. For example, Goldman Sachs doubled its money by funding a successful early childhood education project.[22] However, Goldman Sachs selected that long-running program because it was already a proven success. In its Massachusetts recidivism reduction project, Goldman Sachs employees lobbied juvenile justice workers to attempt to influence the "independent" assessment of success.[23] Pay for Success should be seen largely as a way for private investors to inflate and skim costs of services, driving money out of public coffers and into investment banks while providing lots of well-paying professional class jobs to those in nonprofits, philanthropies, and universities who help put these deals together.

While the websites and press releases of the social impact industry, such as those of bank UBS and rock star Bono, are effusively celebratory of the convergence of Social Impact and AI, others see trouble. Alyson McDowell, a scholar and activist with a widely influential technology and society blog Wrench in the Gears, has been warning about the dangers of the convergence of impact investing and digital technology. She writes,

> "Pay for success" was embedded into federal education law with the passage of the Every Student Succeeds Act. Public-private partnerships, in coordination with investors, are embracing this form of "innovative finance," catalyzing new markets in human capital. Digital platforms, including ed-tech and online behavioral services,

are designed to generate data for the evaluation of outcomes-based contracts. That is what is behind the push for expanded screen-time and benchmark testing in schools. . . . Children are being turned into data so the debt associated with funds allocated to provide education and social services to them can be traded on global markets (like bundled mortgages prior to the 2008 crash).[24]

McDowell's warning needs to be taken seriously, as the varieties of AI education schemes stand to completely displace the humanistic, social, and democratic potential of public education in favor of making students into captured data engines, putting those students on rigid tracks for the future by the very information they are compelled to produce.

SITUATING AI PRIVATIZATION IN THE CONTEXT OF NEOLIBERAL PRIVATIZATION, DE-DEMOCRATIZATION, AND THE LEGACIES OF POSITIVISM

The means of profit through corporeal control expanded radically in the neoliberal era. The for-profit control of bodies ranges from the multibillion-dollar test and textbook standardization craze to the connected multibillion-dollar business in drugging students to enhance test performance and attention with ADHD medications; the massive growth of security apparatus, school militarization and prisonization; and the boom in contracting out the management of schools to corporations facilitated through the charter movement. Since the 2000s, the turn to the body and its control has expanded with a focus on behaviorist social and emotional learning and grit pedagogies particularly promoted through rigid control-oriented private school contractors, such as KIPP and Edison Learning that seek to standardize knowledge, time, and space of school. Old and new forms of social and cultural reproduction and the turn to the body created the conditions for the forms of privatization through digital technology.

AI technologies continue to deepen the repressive and corporeal control trends in neoliberal education. Biometric pedagogy presumes that teaching aims to produce a biological effect that can be measured on the body and its behaviors. In this case, physical response stands in for attention and learning. Teaching becomes a performance that is measured for its impact on the body of the student. Biometric pedagogy uses cutting edge technology for real time data analytics that is supposed to provide the teacher with information about whether students are paying attention or exhibit a "positive valence" toward a lesson. However, biometric pedagogy is radically regressive, dredging up early twentieth-century models of scientific management and Taylorism that aimed for ever-greater amounts of physical measurement of labor and subtasks. Such measurement aims for ever-greater control over the worker's body.

Indeed, it is not a coincidence that biometric surveillance and "nudging" technologies are being implemented in warehouses, factories, and schools. A major casualty of such technologies is the displacement of teaching and learning oriented toward dialogue, interpretation, and judgment. Instead, teaching is conceived as a means of knowledge transfer with the technology facilitating ever-greater efficiencies of delivery. As Williamson points out, the biometric pedagogy trend is wrapped up with the making of social and emotional learning into quantifiable behaviors that are correlated to market capacities of subjects as future workers.[25] Here we see the uses of AI in the making of market-based subjectivity and the development of quantification of subjective representations. Despite being widely promoted as "personalized," adaptive learning tends to delink learning from student and teacher subjectivities and particular contexts as well as from the broader social context. Instead, adaptive learning builds standardization, homogenization, and constant testing into the curriculum and pedagogy.

Moreover, adaptive learning appears to be developing toward a kind of techno-tracking—making a longitudinal case out of the student, interpellating the student through technology use practices into a good or bad, efficacious or failed, student for whom the implicit values, ideologies, and messages of the curriculum are beyond question and debate. Such techno-tracking sorts and sifts students under a false guise of individualized teaching—rewarding the cultural capital of class and culturally dominant students and punishing the cultural capital of class and culturally subordinate students. In their current implementations, these technologies are largely repeating and deepening the worst aspects of standardized testing and its refusal of the cultural politics of knowledge, its mistaken framing of test scores as learning. The tendencies are deeply antidemocratic: They treat knowledge as a consumable commodity rather than as subject to contestation, while undermining learning as the basis for social and political agency. They falsely frame knowledge and school as apolitical.

It is not a coincidence that the profit-seeking activities of privatizers are antidemocratic. To extract profit, businesses impose hierarchical controls even at the expense of productivity.[26] In the case of educational privatization, the standardization and homogenization of curriculum, pedagogical approaches, and school models aims to maximize the possibilities of profit through "economies of scale" and by automating and displacing the most expensive element of schooling: teacher labor. While this tendency for standardization and homogenization of knowledge has been particularly common in for-profit educational management organizations (such as Edison Learning), saving money by using mass-produced curricula, it continues with AI. For example, despite the appropriation of the language of "personalized learning," adaptive learning companies use homogenous curricula and homogenous regular tests with automated adjustments to the pace of delivery. Adaptive learning decontextualizes learning from the subjective experiences of students and the particular cultural knowledge they bring to the learning encounter. Similarly, biometric pedagogy devices aim to measure the impact of delivery of a standardized lesson. Privatization also captures the uses of public institutions for private sector uses and imposes corporate managerial models that ensure that the external private uses of public schools are the priority for public schools over other uses that might directly serve the public interest. A glaring instance of this capture is the way that basic skills and disciplinary agenda for low pay, low skill workers are imposed on the schools of working class and poor communities rather than intellectual and socially engaged forms of teaching that treat knowledge as a form of social agency and instrument for self-governance. The ideologies of corporate culture could not be more apparent than in the case of Mark Zuckerberg's and Summit CEO Dianne Tavenner's description of Summit, where they celebrate students working on their laptops around a table: "According to Zuckerberg, 'it feels like the future—it feels like a start up.' And says Tavenner, 'It looks more like Google or Facebook than a school.'"[27] But where Summit has been most widely implemented, such as Providence, Rhode Island, the technology appears not to feel much like "a start up" and "the future" to teachers, administrators, and students, who resent excessive screen-focused schooling and "almost universally dislike it," feeling bored and burned out, according to an external review of the district by Johns Hopkins researchers.[28] They also found that students skipped lessons to guess on tests, and the technology undermined collective and individual lessons. Though it is hard to discern whether students are learning from their activities, they are nonetheless producing commercially valuable data in their compulsory attendance.

The repressive and deeply antidemocratic tendencies of the neoliberal era[29] mark a significant break with the way that public schooling was implicated in reproducing the social and cultural conditions for capital accumulation in the industrial era. As Bowles and Gintis detailed, in the industrial economy, public schools largely taught class-based knowledge, skills, and dispositions for students to take their prescribed places in the economy as workers or managers. Students learned not just skills and know-how for work but also the ideologies and social relations for them to become sufficiently docile and obedient workers or collaborative and authoritative leaders. Industrial era social and cultural reproduction represented a long-term investment in creating the conditions for workers' labor to be profitable for owners. These conditions included time and labor-intensive learned self-regulation of workers. In the neoliberal era, the offshoring of production, deindustrialization, the shift from the industrial to the financial and service economy, and the end of the grand bargain between capital and labor resulted in a revision of social and cultural reproduction. Social and cultural reproduction in the post-Fordist neoliberal era relies less and less on disciplinary power (that is, learned self-regulation) and more and more on direct control of bodies. Profits in the postindustrial neoliberal economy rely less on long-term investments in making subjects equipped with the knowledge and dispositions for exploitable work. Increasingly, the body and its activity itself becomes a commodity that facilitates contracting profits. From for-profit prisons to for-profit schools, control of bodies becomes a lucrative means for capital accumulation. In this context, the time- and labor-intensive forms of self and social control give way to direct coercive technologies. The process of psychological therapy gives way to the behavior control pill. The rehabilitative prison gives way to warehousing in for-profit prisons. School for work gives way to school for contracting.

Part of what is new with the measurement and control over the body through biometrics, adaptive learning, and Social Impact Bonds is the use of the students' bodies as engines of data production. As Sadowski (2019, 2) points out, data is capital, and digital-technology producers aim to capture as much data as possible for potential future use through Big Data applications. Longstanding school commercialism, such as advertising in textbooks, aims to take advantage of students as a captive audience that is particularly vulnerable to the messages and imprints of corporations hoping to make loyal lifelong consumers. AI education platforms function more akin to what mass communications theorist Dallas Smyth described in relation to advertising-driven broadcast television. Smyth explained that TV ads compel the viewer to do the uncompensated educative labor of learning about products and learning social relations conducing to the reproduction of capital.[30] AI education puts youth to work using applications to create enormous quantities of data about the user, the group of users, and the institution. The data that youth produce has a commercial value that is extracted by the digital technology company, while the data producer is uncompensated. A democratic approach to the ownership and control over data would insist on data makers retaining ownership rights to the data that they produce and reaping any financial benefits to such activity either individually or collectively. A more deeply democratic approach to data would be to recognize that the very concept of data is educationally problematic in that it denies the values, assumptions, and ideologies informing the data and it also denies the values, assumptions, and ideologies of the person interpreting the meaning of data.

Sadowski points out that data is not "mined" but rather manufactured, "a recorded abstraction of the world created and valorised by people using technology."[31] As Sadowski observes, data has become akin to financial capital and is itself a form of capital. Corporations are collecting data first so that they can subsequently figure out what to do with it for profit. What is so troubling about this is that the values and assumptions of data collection are unexamined. The values, assumptions, and ideologies undergirding the design of data collection algorithms are delinked from the data that the use of said algorithms manufacture. Most users lack the technical coding skill, let alone the cultural theory, to deconstruct the AI education platform and recontextualize the data they produce in terms of broader economic, political, and cultural systems, structures, and forces.

Sadowski's point gets to one of the crucial yet largely unexplained aspects of AI education regarding the cultural politics of knowledge. A great deal of criticism about the social uses of AI technology suggests that AI *replicates biases and prejudice.* Such a description, though correct about the replication of injustice, wrongly suggests a potential neutral, unbiased, and objective data production process. Virginia Eubanks' *Automating Inequality* (2017) and Cathy O'Neil's *Weapons of Math Destruction* (2016) both make this point. Eubanks, for example, details how longstanding racist and classist assumptions get built into AI technology that surveils, tracks, and automatically cuts social benefits to profiled recipients. While Eubanks and O'Neil are correct that the technology does this, they mistakenly presume that the technology could be used in a neutral and unbiased way, as if the technology could be outside contested cultural meanings, values, and ideologies. Ruha Benjamin's concept of "The New Jim Code" aims to address this issue. She defines The New Jim Code as "the employment of new technologies that reflect and reproduce existing inequities but that are promoted and perceived as more objective or progressive than the discriminatory systems of a previous era."[32] As she emphasizes, codes operate within systems of meaning.[33] The mistake of thinking that a technology or data can be cleansed of bias makes the false assumption that culture itself can be apolitical. This is similar to the common false assumption that bias can be rooted out of standardized tests to arrive at culturally and politically neutral standardized tests. Data needs to be comprehended as a motivated representation of reality. As Stuart Hall pointed out, representations can never be seen

as merely reflections of reality or merely a function of autho-
rial intent. Representations produce reality; their production,
circulation, economy, subjectivity-producing tendencies, and
interpretations are deeply implicated in relations of power.[34]
The acts of framing and interpreting knowledge depend on
prior values, assumptions, and ideologies that are informed
by the material and symbolic interests and social position of
the one doing the framing and interpreting. Data manufacture
needs to be comprehended as a signifying practice and a part
of representational politics, in which cultural producers are
responsible for the meanings that they make, the ways those
meanings affirm or contest existing broader public discourses,
and the ways those representations create subject positions for
the consumers of those meanings. Contrary to Hall's insights,
both standardized testing and the AI education applications
I have discussed in this chapter are premised on the ideology of positivism, which has a long history of antidemocratic
approaches to education.[35]

The framing of knowledge as "data" (a kind of magical
product delinked from the conditions of its production) continues a longstanding positivist approach to teaching and
learning. The ideology of positivism has played a central role
in both the industrial and neoliberal trends of the ways schooling has been involved in the social and cultural reproduction
of capital. Positivism treats knowledge as a collection of facts
and denies the theoretical assumptions that inform claims to
truth.[36] In the industrial economy, the ideology of positivism
fostered a "hidden curriculum" of capitalism in which, under
the guise of liberal values for the public good and humanism,
the school taught knowledge, skills, dispositions, and ideologies for work.[37] Tests and grades purporting to be neutral, disinterested, objective, and universally valuable were involved in
rewarding the class-based and cultural knowledge of professional class students and punishing that of working class and
nondominant students. Positivism played an important role

in de-democratizing the culture of schools such that the process of teaching and learning would be depoliticized. Positivism conceals the relationships between knowledge and power, and through the guise of disinterested neutrality it imposes the knowledge, values, dispositions, and cultural capital of ruling groups and classes while punishing the knowledge, tastes, and dispositions of oppressed people. Positivism presents truth as a collection of atomized facts, presents knowledge as delinked from the social world, and presents the subject as an atomized consumer of decontextualized fact. In contrast to positivism, democratic schooling would foster a culture of schooling in which knowledge is comprehended in relation to broader questions of power and politics, in which claims to truth are comprehended in relation to broader social antagonisms, and knowledge and learning as social products are seen as forming socially constituted selves.

From the early neoliberal restructuring of education in the 1980s to the present, educational privatization has been characterized by a few key elements that continue with the advent of digital privatization and particularly in the manifestations of AI education: (1) the use of privatization to amass wealth by suppressing teacher wages and transferring that wealth to investors; (2) the de-democratizing shift in political control over schools, curriculum, and pedagogy afforded by privatization from teachers, students, parents, and communities to investors and owners; (3) the pairing of privatization with standardization, homogenization of knowledge, and transmissional, all authoritarian models of pedagogy; (4) the repressive shift in social and cultural reproduction to pillage the public and commodify bodie; and (5) the pairing of privatization with the positivist denial of cultural politics—that is, with democratic conceptions of culture.

Despite the dominant and antidemocratic tendencies in the uses of AI education, there are democratic and progressive pedagogical possibilities in the uses of AI technology evident outside of formal schooling. This suggests possible future directions for the critical uses of AI in schools. For example, The Whitney Biennial in New York in 2019 featured a video art installation, "Triple Chaser" by Forensic Architecture, about an AI project that was designed to teach computers to recognize tear gas grenade canisters manufactured by the company Safariland that were deployed against civilian populations engaged in public dissent and protest around the world. The public pedagogy of the art installation educates viewers about the for-profit activities of the arms manufacturer and its role in governments' violent attacks on civilian populations. The display shows how artists taught computers to recognize the tear gas canisters, how they recruited people around the world to submit images of canisters for computer identification, and they showed video footage of the attacks by police and military. The technology enabled the artists to illuminate the relationships between the state and corporations while showing how the hidden commodity chain can be reconstructed to expose the ways that nation states terrorize populations, including US Border Patrol agents firing tear gas at civilians in Mexico. "Triple Chaser" uses AI to produce data about objects (tear gas cannisters) that gives new meaning to those objects' history, social location, and violent use by interested parties. The investigation expanded to reveal Safariland owner Warren Kanders' financial involvement in the company Sierra Bullets whose bullets were used by the Israeli Defence Forces to fire live ammunition at Palestinians in Gaza. The exhibit also highlighted its own location in relation to the subject matter by revealing that the vice chair of the board of the Whitney Museum, Warren Kanders, is the owner of Safariland.

Forensic Architecture's "Triple Chaser" project built on the work of numerous activist organizations that are part of a broader social movement for global justice, including "Decolonize This Place." In July 2019, in reaction to the social movement and the art exhibit, Kanders resigned from the board of the Whitney. The project illustrates the democratic educative potential of the use of AI technology as part of a broader effort between cultural producers and activists to hold economic and political elites accountable for abuses of power. It suggests the possibilities for using the technology to enable students to comprehend the relationships among learning, knowledge, the self, the society, and the workings of power. Critical pedagogy is a necessary element of such projects. It would allow students to theorize the technology they utilize in ways that comprehend claims to truth in relation to broader social antagonisms; it would also allow them to understand the ways these antagonisms are subjectively experienced. To be used in ways that accord with values for justice and democracy, AI education demands an engagement with representational politics that allows users to comprehend knowledge politically. To use AI education well requires being explicit about the ethical and political norms guiding the use and purpose of the technology and rejecting the quasi-scientific mode of descriptions that obscures the values, politics, interests, and ideologies animating the framing of data and the use of the technology. The technology can be harnessed to democratic education projects, in which the technology aids social interpretation as a means of collective agency to intervene in public problems, to challenge oppressive power, and to foster democratic social relations. However, without adequately comprehending AI education as a form of cultural production and representational politics, AI education stands to continue as the newest incarnation of public sector profiteering by making public schools reliant on expensive technology that only worsens the anti-intellectual and antidemocratic tendencies of the educational reforms that preceded it.

3 NEW DIRECTIONS OF GLOBAL EDUCATIONAL PRIVATIZATION: DIGITAL TECHNOLOGY, SOCIAL AND EMOTIONAL LEARNING, AND THE QUANTIFICATION OF AFFECT

A for-profit social and emotional learning (SEL) program called "Centervention Zoo U" teaches emotional and social skills by putting children in front of games on screens.[1] A for-profit classroom management program, Class Dojo, which is in 80 percent of US schools and 95 percent of K–8 schools, uses behaviorial surveillance to levy disciplinary practices on children while inducing them to generate commercially valuable data. The company uses the data to market lucrative pay for fee at home programs in mindfulness, growth mindset, and other resilience content.[2] A for-profit real time webcam biometric product called "Affdex" measures students' physical movements and translates them into interest and disinterest, and positive and negative valence, and it treats teaching and learning as physiological effects on bodies.[3]

These examples typify a growing global industry in SEL technology products that quantify student behavior, track student data, and allow investors to expand a growing frontier in educational privatization. Despite the lack of strong research evidence for the efficacy of such products, profits are being sought by these companies and investors through selling technology services to public schools, getting students and teachers to produce commercially valuable data, generating enormous profits in social impact bonds, and increasingly securitizing these bonds as speculative investments.[4]

Globally, educational privatization is expanding in new directions that are characterized by the trade in data and digital technologies, the making of students and teachers into data engines, and the use of data and digital technologies to expand impact investment schemes.[5] The quantification of so-called "academic achievement" in the form of standardized testing has long benefited big business, particularly test and textbook companies.[6] Education and technology sectors have been converging as test and textbook publishing education companies like Houghton-Mifflin, ETS, Pearson, and Kaplan have increasingly become technology companies, and technology companies have increasingly become education companies.[7] However, the quantification and datafication of affect, student behavior, learned dispositions particularly for self-control, and so-called "soft-skills" under the rubric of SEL are at the center of the new forms of technology-oriented privatization on a global scale.[8] Such social quantification projects in SEL employ artificial intelligence education technologies, such as adaptive learning technologies, biometric pedagogy devices (like real-time webcam systems), video games, and avatars. The increasing turn to harnessing the daily activities of students, teachers, and administrators as data manufacturers via technology and the financial securitization of this data builds on longstanding dominant trends of profit seeking in education. That is, such technologies displace the labor costs of teachers and allow corporations to capture public education tax dollars by replacing the work and meaning-making activities of teachers with corporate technology in the form of contracting.[9] The trade in and devising of impact investment financial instruments based on student data-making represents a new major source of school profit seeking.[10]

This steady expansion of digital profiteering in public schooling needs to be understood not merely as a consequence of new technologies but rather as part of a broader class-based global project for hegemonic control by the transnational

capitalist class.[11] As William I. Robinson argues, crises of capital overaccumulation and state legitimacy have resulted in
strategies for "militarized accumulation" to expand markets
into hitherto uncolonized places, including the lifeworld and
subjectivity.[12] Globally, public education has been positioned
by ruling class ideologues and profiteers as ripe for economic
pillage. Supranational organizations (e.g., Organisation for
Economic Co-operation and Development (OECD), World Economic Forum, the World Bank), venture philanthropies (The
Bill and Melinda Gates Foundation, The Rockefeller Foundation), and philanthrocapitalist organizations (Chan Zuckerberg
Initiative, Omidyar Network, Emerson Collective), corporate
foundations, consultancies, lobbyists, and think tanks join with
investing banks to form a coordinated movement to fund,
politically influence, and create the ideologies to support the
expansion of educational privatization. Such privatization
shifts ownership and control of schools and education to private actors, siphons money out of the educational process, and
influences content and control of curriculum and pedagogical
approaches. In the United States, public education represents
at least a half trillion dollars a year that can be taken through
privatizations.[13] Some of the better-known forms of these educational privatizations that have continued since the 1980s
include charters; vouchers; scholarship tax credits (tax-based
vouchers); contracting; and the privatization of teacher education, student teaching, and educational leadership.[14] Along
with these dominant privatizations of past decades are others
that are less known. For example, the charter school real estate
and charter bond industries are massive, with predictions of a
potential trillion-dollar charter bond bubble bursting.[15] What
is still less evident to the public is the recent rapid growth
of two major new forms of educational privatization that are
in fact converging: (1) impact investing schemes that promote privatization of education, such as venture philanthropy
and social impact bonds, and (2) data-producing educational

technologies. The specific form of digital capitalist pillage of the lifeworld takes shape as what Nick Couldry and Ulises Meijas refer to as the industries of social quantification.[16] What I am detailing here is the ways that these two forms of privatization, SEL and impact investing, are coming together in part through the quantification of affect and behavior, particularly through the discourse of SEL that is being promoted by supranational organizations, corporations, investors, and philanthropic foundations.

Major surpranational organizations that represent the transnational capitalist class, such as the OECD and the World Economic Forum are leading the trend of actively promoting and developing standards for the quantification of SEL.[17] These supranational organizations as well as such global figures as Bill Gates and a number of large technology companies seized on the COVID-19 pandemic spreading globally in the spring of 2020 to advocate for the global expansion of online learning and to question the return to brick and mortar schooling.[18] Even as, under quarantine, parents around the world got a sudden added appreciation for the hard work that teachers do, such preachers of neoliberal education as Gates, Andrew Cuomo, and Education Secretary Betsy DeVos used the pandemic to advance privatization and the agenda of technology companies, investors, and rightist ideologues of "unbundling" public schooling—that is, transforming it into a collection of discrete private services like cable TV.[19] The "unbundling" and "rethinking education as we know it" agendas have long been an aim discussed in the publications of rightist think tanks.[20]

In part, this chapter seeks to explain and reconcile what superficially appears to be two seemingly contradictory directions of educational reform, policy, and practice between freedom and domination. On one hand, new educational technologies—including artificial intelligence (AI), adaptive learning, biometric pedagogy, blockchain, and the Internet of Things—are promoted by proponents as transforming the process of schooling through promises of freedom from coercion, promises of respect for student individual differences, and learning that is "personalized." These technologies measure, quantify, datafy, and normalize behavior and affect while making student activity into data manufacture.[21]

Such promises of freedom, attention to difference, context, and specificity are framed as overcoming the longstanding standards and accountability movements that have been interwoven with neoliberal educational restructuring. Citizens, parents, and teachers have widely rebelled against the central characteristics of the neoliberal standards and accountability movement that has been in force since 2000. The standards and accountability movement was characterized by "excessive" standardized testing, teaching to the test, standardization and homogenization of curriculum, disregard for student subjectivity, disregard for context, and disregard for culture. Indeed, SEL developed largely in response to these trends. SEL seemingly emphasizes the need to attend to student's subjectivity—a subjectivity largely denied through the objectivistic tendencies of the accountability movement with its revival of the radical empiricist and industrial transmission traditions of education. Radical empiricism framed education as filling the empty vessel with knowledge through ever-greater efficiencies derived from measurement and control.

In the United States, SEL was propelled by the Every Student Succeeds Act (2015) that made nonacademic achievement measures of student progress—a response to public antipathy to excessive testing and standardization expressed in No Child Left Behind (2002) and the Common Core (2010) (laws that were aggressively lobbied into existence respectively by educational test and textbook publishers and Gates). SEL purports to offer remedies to individual psychological and related physical trauma born of violent contexts, providing tools for students to modify their behavior and dispositions.[22] For example, grit pedagogies seek to teach persistence albeit largely through behaviorist techniques; mindfulness and meditation pedagogies teach traumatized students to turn away from hostile contexts and develop peaceful dispositions by focusing inward on the self.[23] Like SEL, new digital technologies, such as CZI's Summit have sought to sell their program in contradistinction from the standards and accountability movement as well. CZI promotes Summit adaptive learning technology through a promise of "personalization," a departure from high stakes testing, and the decentering of the teacher as the locus of knowledge, instead promoting collaborative learning.[24]

However, what has been framed as freedom, individualism, attention to difference is often its opposite: standardized, homogenized, and oriented toward hierarchical modes of authority. For example, despite its promotion as being personalized and sensitive to difference, CZI's Summit disregards student subjectivity, the relationships among learning and student experience and cultural context, and installs constant testing as the mode of pedagogy.[25] This comes in a form that emulates and celebrates corporate culture and the corporate workplace.[26] Or consider biometric analytic pedagogy that promises to offer teachers technological tools to respond to individual student interest and disinterest in a topic by measuring a student's physical response to a lesson. Biometric technology (such as Affdex, recently purchased by IMOTIONS) uses webcams to measure the facial reactions of students and then analyzes and interprets the data as positive or negative valence, attention or disinterest.[27] Despite promising individualization, biometric pedagogy transforms teaching into a scripted performance and evacuates from the learning process thinking, consciousness, and mediation. It models pedagogy on television advertisement market research for physiological excitation.[28] In both of these examples, students generate behavioral data that is of commercial value.

SOCIAL AND EMOTIONAL LEARNING

SEL, while not unitary, is largely characterized by liberal discourse that purports to teach character: self and social awareness, self-control, relationship skills like teamwork and conflict resolution, and "ethical" decision-making skills. SEL encourages resilience to existing social conditions, such as poverty and inequality, and the traumas that they cause. SEL appears to focus on the subjectivity of students. The promise of SEL is one of academic and then social inclusion if only the students can regulate their habits, behavior, and dispositions. SEL programs tend to promote a conception of agency characterized by accommodation to existing social arrangements and institutions rather than transformation of them. SEL programs tend to reject conflict and contestation in favor of valuing consensus-building. But these programs tend to ignore systemic and structural power relations that consensus conceals and that favor groups with more social power.

Though commonly framed as apolitical, SEL does have a politics. The politics of SEL clearly contrasts with the tradition of critical pedagogy that educates youth to analyze, theorize, and criticize structural and systematic forms of oppression and inequality. Critical pedagogy makes learning the basis for reconceptualizing the self and the society and makes such understanding the basis for collective social power. SEL teaches coping skills and dispositions for individual survival in existing institutions and relations of power. SEL programs take seemingly different forms, including (1) learned self-management of emotions; (2) grit pedagogies that are about learned endurance of drudgery, mindfulness/meditation projects that turn focus inward and away from the forces that produce poverty and violence; and (3) "restorative justice" or other conflict resolution programs that seek largely individualized and developmental psychological modes of translating public and political problems into personal problems.[29] These programs

are united by an aim to largely teach economically and culturally oppressed youth self-regulation, social relationships, and
dispositions for submission to authority and for collaboration
in existing social forms and institutions.

Proponents of SEL seek to show that by developing such
specific skills and dispositions, students will have greater
opportunity for traditional academic and then social success.
Significantly, SEL tends to affirm learning and knowledge as
politically neutral. Emotional adjustment serves the transmission of knowledge for work and consumption opportunities
in the market economy. Such a view denies the cultural politics of knowledge and curriculum, and it delinks learning from
self and social transformation. Specifically, SEL programs tend
to deny the relevance of social antagonisms, structural power
relations, and the ways that the self is formed through these
social antagonisms. Consequently, SEL programs tend not
to foster collective political agency that would allow public
problems to be collectively addressed through learning and
experienced as objects of critical analysis. Instead, as in the liberal philosophical tradition, these projects offer individualistic conceptions of agency, delinking learning from its socially
transformative capacity.

The aim of making "resilient" subjects puts the onus for
ameliorating the destruction of structural inequality on the
individual student. Such individualizing of responsibility
for responding to social violence benefits ruling groups and
classes, which do not have to give anything up to create the
social conditions for economic equality, political power shar-
ing, and cultural institutions structured in deeply democratic
ways. More specifically, the new form of character education
allows ruling class people to evade paying for public education
that would give everyone the kind of schools that the richest
have and remedy the historical failure to do so. Worse yet, new
contracting in the technologies of character formation allows
ruling class people to profit from displacing blame onto those

who did not make the conditions in which they suffer and endure. Through learned self-control, the "resilient" student can allegedly be made to withstand the violence of poverty and all of its ancillary effects and to endure symbolic violence that positions them as embodying cultural deficits. As I have argued elsewhere, the discourse of such resilience strategies as "grit" needs to be understood as neoliberal character education in an era characterized by shifting the burden for social service provision onto individuals.[30]

DATA PRIVATIZATION, IMPACT INVESTING, AND THE QUANTIFICATION OF SEL

Ben Williamson and Nelli Piattoeva have detailed how the OECD has worked to standardize SEL definitions and standards in order to create the conditions for it to be quantified and datafied.[31] Williamson and Piattoeva explain that the OECD and the World Economic Forum aim to stabilize the field of knowledge as a supposed natural science about SEL and create a new policy consensus and common sense about it by drawing together concepts from psychology and economics. Key figures who have promoted neoliberal human capital theory, such as James Heckman, are now promoting the quantification of SEL. Williamson and Piattoeva point out that a central aspect of this project involves establishing bounded norms of selfhood in psychological categories.[32]

Williamson and Piattoeva study how organizations promoting SEL work with the OECD to create categories and technologies to measure and quantify SEL. These authors decry the false claims to objectivity in the discursive production of SEL: "Our main claim is that SELS, as a contested science in the making, embodies attempts by policy influencers to stabilize the field through the production of objectivity, while broadening and consolidating the uses of education technology." As Williamson and Piattoeva rightly point out, claims to objectivity "focus on expelling subjectivity."[33] The objectivizing of SEL is a class and cultural project of ruling groups to secure their hegemony by legitimation. The elaborate use of positivist ideology in technology is about securing social power as well as cultural dominance. Perhaps the greatest material interest in objectivizing SEL is to translate it into commercially viable data for those who own and invest in educational technology industries.

The OECD and World Economic Forum reports, websites, and documents show a number of key framing assumptions about the linkage between SEL and data manufacture. Among these are: (1) The need for more "private sector involvement" in public education, including public–private partnerships and private financing and investment.[34] This presumes that technology corporations and banks need to play a greater role in SEL and its quantification; (2) The alignment of human capital (education as a market-based investment that pays off in expanded labor markets, capitalist growth, and global economic competition) with "psycho-informatics" (techniques and technologies that measure, datafy, track, and analyse behavior, affect, and dispositions, such as biometric analytic technologies).[35] (3) The need for SEL to be datafied.[36] (4) A view of globalization and technology as the key drivers of change akin to natural forces producing inequality. Such a perspective does not recognize the extent of class antagonism, domination, and hegemonic struggle.[37] In this view, individual agency takes shape as resilience compelled by "forces of nature." "Resilience" thinking does not recognize the extent to which particular versions of globalization (global justice movement versus neoliberal globalization) or technology (technology as a tool for equality and freedom from domination versus technophilic capitalism) are collective human products, ideological formations that are far from natural or inevitable, and for their propagation require being continuously taught and learned; and (5) The so-called "soft skills" promoted by SEL as crucial for economic development and the new directions of industry in the "4th Industrial Revolution."[38]

In addition to key framing assumptions, the supranational organizations share certain key constitutive absences that frame their projects. These absences include a tendency to gut educational and social theory and humanities traditions from the discussion of what is needed in schools and society. Instead, these organizations pair up psychological developmental tropes from empiricist traditions with positivist measures of learning expressed through standardized testing. This produces a particular version of the relationship between individual subjects and knowledge in which individual experiences are valuable in relation to learning only as a means of comprehending the proper dispositions for the consumption of knowledge or of comprehending blockages to the efficient consumption of knowledge formed by "bad" habits or trauma.

In contrast to critical pedagogy, the goal of SEL is not to develop in students the capacity to theorize claims to truth, the self, or the social in relation to authority.[39] Nor is the aim to comprehend the politics of knowledge, the extent to which the self is socially formed, or the contextual dimensions of truth claims in the service of collective forms of self-governance and social agency.[40] That is, SEL has been largely organized to deny contests over curriculum, pedagogical approaches, symbolics, interests, and ideologies. This aspect of SEL, which draws on empiricist and developmentalist forms of psychology while eschewing the politics of education, has to be recognized as a political framing that largely expresses liberal ideologies of education—the impossible claim that knowledge and curriculum are apolitical and must be framed as "neutral."[41] Consistent with the denial of the politics of knowledge and curriculum, the World Economic Forum asserts that children should learn to approach problems "the way a computer would."[42] In this view, all problems are technical problems and practical problems, not matters of interpretation and judgment. Such a view presumes that there is no place for critical questions about the relationship between the framing of problems and the interests, ideologies, and social locations of specific groups of people. Yet the crucial innovation of the latest push for SEL quantification and measurement is its connection to the industry in digital technology contracting, the trade in data, and the continuing growth of impact investing schemes. In chapter 4, I develop this discussion to consider how the quantification and commercialization of affect is being developed through the play-based learning movement coordinated by supranational organizations and corporations. In chapter 6, I return to the Williamson and Piattoeva analysis of the OECD's objectivizing of a quasi-science of SEL in relation to rising distrust of specialists and expert knowledge, and I complicate their political analysis.

IMPACT INVESTING

SEL is not the only mechanism espoused by educational world policy to privatize education on a global scale. In addition to longstanding neoliberal privatization schemes, such as vouchers, charters, and scholarship tax credits, innovative education financing has more recently been taking the form of impact investing.

For example, an early childhood education program in Chicago that was already established as a success was funded by Goldman Sachs with $16.9 million. After the evaluation deemed the program a success, Goldman was paid $30 million by Chicago, allowing the bank to keep the difference.[43] Such public–private partnerships appear to be private sector shakedown schemes. Social Impact Bonds have banks pay for the service, and if the program is deemed successful, then the government pays the bank back with significant additional money. The philanthropies help set up the deals and often are involved in arranging evaluation of the programs.

Proponents of Social Impact Bonds claim that these schemes are more accountable than direct government provision of services because of these evaluations. Critics suggest that the schemes inflate the costs of already successful programs, allowing banks to bilk the public sector while influencing the program evaluations. Critics also suggest that banks cherry pick already successful programs to increase the likelihood of success and hence profit taking. Social Impact Bonds depend upon accountability metrics, and new forms of digital education technology such as AI, Internet of Things, and blockchain are becoming the means to expand SIBs. The quantification of SEL is being positioned to facilitate these automated metrics.

Educational privatization is expanding significantly in the area of the spread of for-profit digital technology in classrooms. This has several implications for educational finance. Cyber school companies such as K12, Inc. have functioned as Educational Management Organizations, running schools for profit particularly by displacing teachers with technology. Conventional measures of quality reveal extremely low performance for cyber schools[44] with the COVID-19 pandemic reaffirming previous concerns about quality and access. Yet, the World Economic Forum used the pandemic as an opportunity to promote its pre- COVID-19 agenda.

Technology companies such as Google, Apple, Microsoft, CZI, Emerson Collective, and Omidyar Network have managed to get hardware, software, and adaptive learning technology into schools. Technology outfits stand to fulfill a rightist dream of ending the very conception of the public school and replacing it with collections of private educational services—that is, "unbundling" the school.[45] These companies are promoting adaptive learning technologies that frame teachers as technology facilitators. In a financial sense this stands to allow technology companies to hijack the role of teachers and their salaries regardless of the lack of efficacy established by these experimental approaches to teaching. As well, a new and massive industry in data capture has opened with the introduction of such technology based learning platforms in schools.[46] CZI for example, is acquiring for profit education companies to expand its cache of student data.[47] Data capture companies are doing an end run around student privacy as third party users of data are not held accountable to youth privacy laws.[48] As adaptive learning technology makes a case of each student it also sorts and sifts students in a new form of techno-tracking.

The latter two "innovative" finance schemes of digital surveillance (facilitated by the quantification and datafication of Social Emotional Learning) and impact investing appear to be converging as impact investors increasingly rely upon digital surveillance to measure and track youth who are rendered into investment commodities. A clear example of this convergence is illustrated by the funding projects of the New Schools Venture Fund, a non-profit organization started by billionaire venture capitalist John Doerr who was an early financier of Google and Amazon.[49] Doerr's NSVF was a major player in promoting prior yet ongoing forms of educational privatization like charter schooling on the model of venture philanthropy.[50] New Schools Venture Fund provides start-up money to mostly for-profit companies contracting with public schools. New School Venture Fund lists 117 educational technology ventures on their website. Forty-three businesses that NSVF funds or has funded are for-profit Social Emotional Learning companies. One such company, Centervention (slogan "Focus on Fun because Fun Works") produces SEL games such as Zoo U that claims to teach students to overcome "extreme reactions to trivial problems," blurting out in class, and to help students "who have trouble making friends."[51] The solution does not involve learning to engage in human interactions with adults and peers. Rather, setting the child in front of a screen for video games will allegedly foster "six key social and emotional skills: communication, cooperation, emotion regulation, empathy, impulse control, social initiation"[52] that will cure all non-conforming "bad" behavior.

Perhaps what is most troubling about the corporate capture of time and teacher student interaction in this case is that such games provide students and teachers no investigation of why a particular student might be having these issues or of how the student's cultural identity and the social and cultural context inform and produce the problem. The SEL product is made meaningful to the student through therapeutic gamification and play instead of via a focus on a student's actual experiences or the social and cultural context. Gamification and play in SEL are values promoted by the World Economic Forum and the LEGO Foundation.

An entire extremely secretive and extremely underregulated industry of student-data brokers acquires student data from such programs and sells it to advertisers and corporations.[53] The data, compelled from uncompensated students using programs of questionable educational value, is then used to market to and manipulate these same youth. As students labor in schools and sometimes at home generating data that is of real commercial value to tech companies in the present, they do so on the dubious future promise that the programs they use may one day allow them to compete to work and consume in exclusionary economic arrangements.

According to the World Economic Forum, the new digital capitalism in education can teach children "positive examples of global citizenship." The World Economic Forum invites children to learn from the Business Roundtable's social impact initiatives: "Businesses can also provide children positive examples of global citizenship. The recent announcement from the US Business Roundtable on stakeholder capitalism provides an opportunity for companies to lead by example and invite children to learn from their social impact initiatives."[54] In realty, this educational activity produces a vision of global citizenship defined less by global justice and learning for shared political agency and control over social life and more by acquiescence to the world as it is. The image of the world such educational strategies give to students is one of consolidating wealth, growing economic inequality, oligarchic government, and cultures of titillating diversion from urgent public matters rather than democratic political, economic, and cultural formations.

MILITARIZED ACCUMULATION, REPRESSIVE EDUCATION, AND "INNOVATIVE FINANCE"

The convergence of digital technology and SEL needs to be understood in relation to broader political economic shifts. The past decade has seen the emergence of two seemingly contradictory trends in education. As I detailed in *Scripted Bodies*, educational repression has been steadily expanding and needs to be understood in relation not merely to the repressive tendencies of neoliberal ideology but also to the economic imperatives of capital accumulation.[55] As William I. Robinson argues, crises of capital accumulation and crises of system legitimacy are reconciled by "militarized accumulation."[56]

During industrial capitalism until the 1980s, public education served as a resource for ruling class people by creating an exploitable labor force and inculcating future workers with ideologies conducive to class domination. The possibilities for profit largely came from forging an exploitable labor force. The ideological formation of the era has been referred to as the "hidden curriculum" of capitalism, in which schooling conferred key beliefs and dispositions that contributed to both the social relations for capital accumulation and the concealment of the hierarchical class relations behind the public education system.[57]

In the 1980s, the neoliberal restructuring of public education brought capitalist interests to the fore as the role and purposes of schooling for work, consumption, and national economic competition became overt justifications for schooling. Neoliberal education created the conditions for profit taking through privatization of schools, contracting, and commercialism. Ideologically, neoliberal education openly rationalized all aspects of schooling through the language and logic of business, consumer choice, and competition. School for work and consumption as well as learning for earning had to be quantifiably measurable. The neoliberal era amplified aspects of the logic of industrial production, scientific management, and positivist ideology with regard to knowledge and curriculum. In addition, its fetish for quantifiable controls aims for ever-greater efficiencies by ubiquitous testing, reducing the measure of teacher quality to student test scores, and discounting those aspects of humanity that do not translate into commerce (e.g., STEM and career and technical education).

The corporatization and militarization of schools expanded throughout the 1990s as the hierarchical and authoritarian organization of the corporation became the model for schools and their administrators. Repressive trends integral to the neoliberal restructuring of schools included standardization of time and space, a revival of largely discredited repressive pedagogies like behaviorism, and security apparatuses in schools. Charter schools that targeted working class and poor, historically disinvested communities (and especially black and brown students) tended and still tend to embrace repressive school models. As Nancy Fraser points out, social and cultural reproduction was revised in the post-Fordist era. Fordist modes of self- and social control, such as learned self-regulation, have increasingly given way to direct coercion in the post-Fordist era.[58] As a result, in education, much of the learned self-regulation (Foucault's discipline) taught in schools for submission to authority in the workplace has given way to coercion: behavior and mood control drugs; school militarization/prisonization; scripted lessons; and standardization of knowledge, time, and space.

In the past decade, prior repressive and neoliberal tendencies have been developed and carried forward through new technologies and new techniques of control: neoliberal character education in the form of grit; biometric pedagogy that teaches the body while discounting the mind; tech-based SEL programs that merge character education with tracking, surveillance, and case-making; the making of students into financial securities through impact bond investments that create investment opportunities out of the behavioral profiling and the sorting and sifting of students.

Schools are not merely places for the ruling class to create profit opportunities and ideological indoctrination. Schools continue to be sites and stakes of ideological and material struggle implicated in producing ideologies and common sense, identity positions, and social relations. Progressive and radical schooling traditions were developed during the Fordist era, as well as during the neoliberal era. The new phase of digital privatization demands new directions for the making of emancipatory ideologies, identifications, and social relations. A number of important directions can be developed. It is crucial for critical scholars to challenge the assumptions about the self and learning undergirding dominant conceptions of SEL. The struggle against the standards and accountability movement and the neoliberal "global education reform movement" that it is part of can be countered with pedagogies that are not grounded in developmental psychology but rather in critical theories and critical pedagogical traditions. Though often developed with vestiges of positivism, behaviorism, or scientific management, new technologies do not have to be embedded in these same worldviews. New technologies can be put in the service of emancipatory ideologies, and egalitarian social relations can be taught through the use of technologies.[59]

Pedagogies that take seriously emotion as a starting point can make central a dialectical conception of the self and the social informed by critical pedagogy and critical theory more generally. Such a perspective would recognize that knowledge, curriculum, and pedagogy are contested and that these contests are informed by broader social, economic, political, and cultural antagonisms. As well, unlike SEL, critical pedagogy recognizes that the self is constructed through social antagonisms and that the self in turn forms the social through both reconceptualizing experience and acting on the world. In this view, learning is a practice of self and social ongoing interpretation and analysis. Such interpretation and analysis draws on a number of humanities, social science, and scientific traditions to allow students to comprehend the relationships between learning and social authority, claims to truth and material and symbolic power. Learning in such a view is a means not merely of adaptation to the existing social world but as primarily a tool to shape and transform the world. Finally, such critical pedagogy cannot be seen as merely an educational methodology or an abstract quantity but needs to be comprehended as part of broader social movements for the advance of democratic culture. Such movement necessitates a staunch rejection of the privatization of public education and instead articulates with a reinvigorated commitment to public forms of governance and control, public investment and ownership, and a commitment to forms of education that can foster democratic cultures in all institutions.

4 THE LEGO FOUNDATION AND THE QUANTIFICATION OF PLAY

Supranational organizations, corporate philanthropies, and corporations have been promoting play-based learning and the quantification of play-based learning. One corporate philanthropy in particular, The LEGO Foundation, which is part of the Real Play Coalition, has been working with the World Economic Forum and the Organisation of Economic Co-operation and Development (OECD) to support the expansion of the measurement, quantification, and assessment of play. The LEGO Group, headquartered in Denmark, is the largest toy company in the world, earning nearly $2 billion a year through sales of its plastic interlocking blocks and also its LEGOLAND theme parks, a series of highly lucrative Hollywood movies, and other merchandise. The LEGO Foundation, a nonprofit organization funded by the company, plays a prominent role in promoting play-based learning internationally. The foundation promoting the idea of an international educational skills crisis that ought to be met with play-based learning. It encourages the measurement and assessment of play, the inclusion of such assessments in the OECD Program for International Student Assessment (PISA) international educational comparison tests, and the linkage of quantified play to the United Nations Millenium Development Goals promoted by the World Bank.[1]

The LEGO Group has not been able to rely on a monopoly over the manufacture of plastic bricks. It faces competition from inexpensive Chinese imitators, whose bricks fit LEGOs. For more than a decade, LEGO has branched out into merchandising tie-ins, partnering with both DC Comics and Marvel Comics on LEGO Super Heroes toys, movies, and video games. They also partner with Pixar on "The Incredibles" franchise, Disney, Warner Brothers, Universal Pictures on Minions, and Minecraft, among many large media corporations. Although to a lesser extent, LEGO sells classic sets of bricks without instructions, LEGO toys have increasingly moved toward providing premade cinematic and video game narratives for themed toys that interlock corporate branding and merchandising arrangements with their products. LEGO sets have concomitantly moved toward instructional kit building with step-by-step instructions for children to build branded toys (DC Comics Batman, Disney scenes, etc.) and moved away from open play. As critics of school commercialism have contended, commercial film franchise tie-ins result in greater prescribed play by children.[2] Critics argue that prescribed play undermines imagination, as children are observed imitating and repeating the narratives and ideologies learned from movies or television rather than creating their own narratives.[3] In addition, the increase in the sale of instructional kits results in the promotion of rule-following to complete an object of someone else's imagining. This tendency of LEGO toys coheres with the LEGO Foundation's promotion of instrumental, skills-developing, practical forms of play. The LEGO website and the Apple App store, appear to be increasingly promoting the interface of branded toy kits with video game apps. These digital directions for LEGO suggest the growing importance for the company of capturing and commercializing the data that children produce through the use of its products.

At the very least, the quantification of play for the LEGO Group has two important dimensions. On one hand, by inserting play into the global accountability and standards movement spearheaded by the supranational organizations OECD and World Economic Forum that represent multinational capital, LEGO aims to position its business and products as essential to educational provision, human development, economic growth, and the acquisition of individual skills that contribute to that economic growth.[4] By promoting play as quantifiable, measurable, and integral to global educational comparisons, LEGO stands to legitimate itself and its profit seeking activities in these regards while increasing the likelihood of greater revenue.

If quantified play can be successfully integrated into global comparative educational accountability standards, then play will be measured along with other academic achievement on national tests that form the basis for international comparisons. OECD wields major soft power influence on national policy around the world as nations seek to follow trends and advice to demonstrate global competitiveness and development to other nations. Nationally, efforts will be made to increase test scores by focusing on the skills and dispositions that will be measured. Having successfully lobbied for the incorporation of play-based learning as a measurable skill, LEGO will be ready to provide the curriculum materials in the form of LEGO products. The LEGO Foundation is heavily investing in its work with other organizations to accomplish this legitimation project: Project Zero at Harvard University, MIT Media Lab, collaborations with OECD, World Economic Forum, and the Real Play Coalition to name a few of the most prominent. Secondly, the agenda for the quantification of play creates the conditions for the increasing convergence of education and media entertainment corporations around digital learning products. This convergence of education and digital media entertainment naturalizes as necessary for learning and human development gamified forms of pedagogy typified in digital social and emotional learning apps, biometric measurement systems, personalized learning products, and the interface of physical toys like LEGOs and drones with digital apps. As well, this convergence creates the conditions for the ever-greater digital measurement and surveillance of children's activity and human activity, the normalization and "making innocent" of total surveillance and commercialization of that surveillance through the discourse of childhood innocence.[5] The expansion of commercialized surveillance is also made to appear innocuous by trading on sentimentality and nostalgia, as nearly every adult has played with LEGO blocks as a child, and the durability of LEGOs in culture makes it seem to be affixed to childhood itself.[6] Such digital surveillance and commercialism includes children's use of screens on various devices and webcams but also the use of biometric tracking devices that are now being put on children in some schools throughout the day, as evidenced in Wildflower Montessori School's tracking of young children's every movement.[7] The social control and commercial extraction/digital representation possibilities of datafication are part of a broader trend toward the "Internet of Things" that aims to integrate the physical world with the internet and digital industry.[8]

This chapter considers the mutual interest of LEGO and supranational organizations in quantifying play and promoting the quantification of play-based learning. What is important to grasp at the outset is how the agenda for play-based learning fits in with the broader trend toward career and technical education (CTE) that is promoted by supranational organizations and the global corporations whose interests they represent.[9] CTE is the latest version of a very longstanding business agenda for education that pushes public schools to teach basic skills for work.[10] CTE runs contrary to humanistic and democratic visions and values for public education that aim to make learning the basis for social understanding and collective political agency. CTE also promotes direct involvement of corporations in the making of curriculum and a vision of public schooling as worker training. LEGO and the OECD/World Bank/World Economic Forum vision for learning through play shares with CTE a central focus on play for work-oriented skill development. In the reports and promotional materials of the LEGO Foundation, OECD, and the World Economic Forum, play for skill development lays claim to specific versions of play, creativity, context, and learning for agency. As I detail later in this chapter, what is misleading in this literature is that language and concepts from progressive educational traditions are being appropriated for a vision consisting of an emphasis on vocational skills, human capital development, and school to work—a vision championed by the representatives of global corporations and the corporations themselves. The incorporation of progressive and critical educational concepts and traditions into the language and logic of business is diametrically opposed to the humanistic origins and values of these terms. In addition, such a shift undermines the public and radically democratic potential of educational practice.

Like the trend for social and emotional learning, the play-based learning movement appears as a reaction against and remedy for the standards and accountability movement of the past several decades. The standards and accountability movement has been characterized by a pedagogical approach dominated by extensive testing and teaching to the test, alignment of practice with a homogenized curriculum, a content delivery/ transmission model of teaching and learning, drudgery, and scripted lessons. Through an emphasis on play, creativity, and meaningful learning, LEGO appears to promote a pedagogy that breaks with the tendencies toward skill and drill, drudgery, and decontextualized meaningless consumption of knowledge of the standards and accountability movement. The LEGO Foundation and the play-based learning movement aims to *objectivize, universalize, and claim as neutral* what are in fact interested concepts, standards, and practices about play, learning, the self, and society that tend to represent the particular values, interests, and ideological perspectives of dominant classes and cultural groups.[11] The play-based learning movement appears as an *almost* progressive pedagogical approach in its assertions about what should be standardized norms for play-based learning globally. According to the literature produced by LEGO Foundation and the Real Play Coalition, the movement emphasizes student pleasure and meaning, a valuation of context and student agency, creativity, and imagination.[12]

However, play-based learning as promoted by LEGO Foundation has particular definitions of context, creativity, imagination, and agency that delink learning from the social, political, cultural, economic, and historical forces and structures that inform children's play, the meanings of play, and the approaches to pedagogy that LEGO promotes. In what follows, I first detail the ways that LEGO Foundation lays particular claim to context, agency, creativity, and imagination. I then situate these definitions in terms of broader economic, political, cultural, and pedagogical realities; social contests; and structures. What becomes apparent in such an analysis is the ways that LEGO/OECD/World Economic Forum agenda promotes a conception of play that aligns with corporate interests and ideologies and stands starkly at odds with public and more radically democratic aspirations for education yet denies the politics of the play-based learning project. This should come as no surprise from a corporation or from supranational organizations dedicated to furthering the interests of global corporations. The justifications for and promotions of play-based learning could be grounded in theoretical perspectives and traditions. However, the selective appropriation of language and concepts from the traditions of progressive and critical education demands particular scrutiny when they are employed in a perspective that largely runs counter to the aims of critical education.

To grasp the play-based learning objectivization project promoted by the LEGO Foundation, LEGO Group, OECD, and World Economic Forum, I examine multiple reports that these organizations produced and distributed, sometimes with partner organizations. I highlight the differences between the central assertions of the play-based movement and the critical educational traditions from which many of the concepts were extrapolated.

PLAY-BASED LEARNING: REDEFINING CONTEXT, AGENCY, CREATIVITY, AND IMAGINATION

LEGO Foundation reports, white papers, working papers, and "leaflets" make the case for play-based learning to be incorporated into global educational standards and for new metrics to be developed to evaluate play-based learning.[13] Along these lines, one of the projects of the LEGO Foundation is to promote play in poor nations where children are "affected by crisis." The LEGO Foundation website features the humanitarian work of the foundation with pictures of Syrian and Rohingya refugees. The accompanying text reads:

> The LEGO Foundation is committed to promote learning through play for children affected by crisis to address a pressing challenge of our time and change the way the world thinks about play and learning through play and its importance for young children in crisis settings.[14]

Similarly, LEGO Foundation does international development projects in poor nations.

The humanitarian interventions by LEGO succinctly illustrate some key elements in the broader project to lobby for play-based learning globally as central to child development, humanitarian intervention, and education. These elements include psychological developmentalist justifications for play-based learning, a claim that student differences and cultural differences matter, that learning should be "meaningful," "engaging," "socially interactive," fostering "agency," supporting "creativity," expanding "imagination," and "socially interactive."[15]

LEGO Foundation and their academic partners "identified five essential characteristics of playful learning, namely joy, meaning, active engagement, social interaction, and itera- tion."[16] What unifies these essential characteristics of play- based learning is an approach to learning and play that delinks individual activity and understanding from the broader social world and specifically from the broader structures, systems, and antagonisms that inform how meaning is socially pro- duced. For example, LEGO defines meaningful play as "when they [teachers] integrate learners' experiences from home and school." While nodding to play being "culturally relevant," play-based learning is made meaningful not by relating the object of knowledge to the broader social context but rather through formal pedagogical techniques that are specific to the classroom setting, like "group reflection on learning, and scaffolding—guiding learners from what is known to what is unknown; from the concrete to the abstract."[17] This reduction of meaning to the local and the evacuation of social context from meaning appear in many of the documents. For exam- ple, Ben Mardell, Daniel Wilson, Jen Ryan, Katie Ertel, Mara Drechevsky, and Megina Baker in the white paper "Towards a Pedagogy of Play" similarly extol the virtues of meaning- ful learning being impacted by "larger forces," yet they define these "larger forces" not as social structures, class antagonisms, or institutional forces but rather as things that are not larger forces at all: "the materials available in the classroom, time, opportunities for learning to interact with each other and class- room and school norms."[18]

Despite the rhetoric of learning being meaningful, contex- tual, and social, play-based learning literature lacks any sense of how the broader social world and its economic, political, and cultural contests and power struggles inform the lived experiences of students and structure the meanings of expe- riences in particular contexts. LEGO Foundation's play-based learning interventions in poor countries and with refugees are positioned on their website as responding to the trauma of collective displacement. Yet play-based learning in this discourse provides no basis for engaging with such students about the subjective traumas they have experienced or the objective forces that produced those subjective experience. Nor is there any sense in this pedagogy of how the act of learning through play or any other way could be the basis for changing an understanding of experience, theorizing experience, making a different meaning of experience by problematizing that experience or comprehending it in relation to broader social realities and traditions of thought.

Play-based learning literature like the "Learning through Play at School" white paper invokes "authentic experience" as that which makes learning meaningful.[19] On the contrary, critical educational traditions recognize that individual experience is never transparently true or authentic but rather always ideological, political, and dependent on interpretation. Experience is mediated through values, assumptions, and sets of meanings that have to be taught and learned for experience to become meaningful. Play-based learning literature celebrates "giving voice and choice" to experiences of joy, pleasure, delight, wonder, and familiar culture.[20]

Critical education traditions seek to expand student agency by fostering the capacity for learning and knowledge to become the basis for social action and intervention and to enable acts of social and self-interpretation and self-governance. Traditions, such as critical pedagogy, provide students with conceptual tools to interpret and problematize knowledge and experience. Contrary to this approach, the LEGO Foundation claims that play-based learning fosters "agency" but positions agency in a strictly affirmational way that both undercuts the critical, socially interpretive, dialogic, and reflective aspects of learning. Agency in this framing is about teaching methodologies, not about learning as the basis for comprehending the social world or the capacity to make such comprehension the basis for acting on and impacting the social world. As a methodology, agency in this discourse is about giving students greater freedom of movement and task choices: "teachers offered some degree of learner choice and voice around carefully planned, managed and assessed rigorous tasks."[21] Play-based learning is a methodological reform announced as a better, softer, and kinder mode of standards and accountability intended to create greater efficiencies of delivery of knowledge: "The promise of such a pedagogy is that it will enable self-directed learning to thrive within the constraints of a schedule, honor children's interests and passions within a context of targeted learning goals and standards-based curriculum, and provide schools with structures that encourage healthy risk-taking while keeping children safe."[22] Play-based learning as promoted by LEGO Foundation is not advocated as a means for students to open up questions about the relationships between knowledge claims and social authority or knowledge as a means of social and political agency. Nor is it an approach to learning that recognizes that knowledge is made dynamically through dialogic exchange. It is instead an instructional methodology for the transmission of "standards-based curriculum."

The absence of a political, critical, and reflective dimension to this form of play-based learning means that children are deprived of an approach to learning that helps them understand what broader social, political, cultural, and economic forces have rendered them less safe (particularly in the contexts of humanitarian crises such as those targeted by LEGO Foundation's projects in refugee camps with children fleeing Syria and Myanmar). After defining play-based learning as a depoliticized pedagogy that can foster dispositions of choice and problem solving, Mardell, Wilson, Ryan, Ertel, Drechevsky, and Baker (2016) suggest that this will position children to address the world's problem and crises.[23] As much of the literature suggests, the experience of refugee children

is traumatic. Yet play-based learning is not positioned as a pedagogical opportunity or entry point to comprehend the social
forces that produce the subjective experience of trauma, displacement, and violence. In the LEGO literature, social context is given as a reason for the need for play-based learning,
but social context is not part of play-based pedagogy itself
(p. 11). So international development work promoting play-
based education does not address the causes of the war and
poverty suffered by the recipients of the LEGO largesse. In this
view, pedagogy is not about comprehending reality to act on
and shape it. Instead it is a methodology to develop problem-
solving skills that maybe one day can be employed to address
broad social problems. This massive disconnection between
experience and the social world and between broader social
problems and pedagogy is at the center of LEGO's version of
play-based learning. This selective reference to LEGO's attention to context and meaning depoliticize pedagogy, reducing
learning to play as a methodology of efficacious delivery of
standardized content and discreet skill.

Sometimes the depoliticization of pedagogy in the LEGO literature overtly makes democracy a methodology: democracy
is a classroom practice, a type of personal interaction among
individuals, not the basis for reconstructing social institutions.
"Knowledge construction in a playful participatory approach
is a democratic process in which the whole school community (e.g., teachers, children, administrators, families) act as
co-researchers (in varying roles and situations), engaging in
both the consumption and production of knowledge."[24] What
is missing here is a sense of how the production of knowledge
and consumption of knowledge are political outside school.
The political economy of knowledge production involves
the vast sums of money and questions of ownership over
meaning-making industries, such as LEGO's brand-interlocking
entertainment narratives. The cultural politics of knowledge
production involves contests and struggles over meanings and

the relationships between the social locations and ideological convictions of specific meaning-making actors. Play-based learning as described by LEGO has no sense of how a democratic approach to learning would have to involve these key questions of the power to make meaning and own meaning-making machinery. Such glaring omissions when discussing democratic pedagogy mean that, for example, the role of global corporations like the LEGO Group as a cultural producer and the student as cultural consumer of their products remain outside the purview of the play-based learning approach. There is no sense here of how students might employ the tools of critical media literacy to analyze and interpret the narratives and ideologies in LEGO's movies, streaming content, and apps.

Delivery, efficiency, and the continuation of standards-based accountability are consistent with the project to incorporate play-based learning into the global standards and accountability movement led by the OECD and to define creativity and imagination through the discourse of skill development for work. LEGO Foundation's literature hence puts out documents calling for creativity and imagination to be quantified and assessed for skill development:[25]

> Why now? It is more important than ever that we are able to have a nuanced and productive conversation about creativity assessment, because the Programme for International Student Assessment (PISA) has selected Creative Thinking as the innovative domain for the 2021 testing cycle—in other words, the creative thinking of teenagers around the world is about to be measured and likely compared.[26]

LEGO is in the business of getting children to consume branded mass media products. LEGO's claims about play-based learning fostering creativity are largely framed through the language of worker training and the move to shift education to "lifelong learning"—another way of describing the trend toward credentialing, in which constant worker training becomes a new normal and education becomes a business for the workplace:

"At the LEGO Foundation, we want to build a future where learning through play empowers children to become creative, engaged lifelong learners. In an age of rapid innovation, where children will encounter unimagined advances and navigate unpredictable dilemmas, this aim is more important than ever before."[27]

This quote begins the LEGO Foundation leaflet "What We Mean by Creativity." The document asserts that creativity in play-based learning should be "iterative," by which they mean experimental. The child tries new possibilities with concrete objects and creates hypotheses about the situation. In this view, creativity is a practical activity with a specific process: "This focus on process aligns with our view that creativity is a skill that can be nourished and practiced."[28] The point not to be missed in the LEGO Foundation framing of creativity is that creativity is about manipulating concrete objects in the present, not about imagining something different. The narrative about creativity sounds strikingly similar to a description of using LEGOs and putting together LEGO kits: "By interacting with the world around them, they connect (link or combine two or more things), explore (adapt, or go one or more steps further) and transform (radically change) ideas and products that already exist around them."[29]

Lest there be any confusion that creativity is about putting together LEGOs, three pages later, a large graphic of three connected LEGOs has the heading "The Creative Process." Each LEGO of the creative process has a title: "Exploring," "Transforming," "Connecting." Subsequent pages of the document put words around images of large LEGOs. What is striking here is not only the unveiled advertisement of the LEGO Group's product under the guise of promoting an allegedly universally beneficial pedagogical approach. What is also striking is that the product being sold informs the definition of creativity put forward in the documents. Creativity is defined through the manipulation of the immediately experienced concrete object (in this case, plastic bricks that are interwoven with Holly-wood commercial content), not through imagining something radically different from what is known and experienced first-hand. "By trying out and developing things that are new to them in everyday contexts, creators learn about their world and gain practice taking risks in a safe environment."[30] What "risks" would the LEGO Foundation be referring to? The risks of putting together colorful bricks? Certainly they are not refer-ring to the risks of being a refugee in flight from a war zone or the risks of attempting to start a new life in a new context. This definition of creativity that limits imagination to the directly experienced and immediately familiar context goes hand in hand with the denial of the broader social context in the play-based learning discourse. In addition, the reduction of creativity to manipulation and experimentation with the concrete ties in with the CTE movement and global standards and accountability movement to reduce schooling to be only about preparation for work. It also justifies the project of sell-ing LEGOs to the world under the guise of education.

In this view, creativity should not be comprehended socially, historically, or culturally. LEGO represents play and the objects of play as outside the broader social and cultural meanings that make objects of play intelligible and desirable. It is as if the political and ideological forces that make some things meaningful in a particular context do not exist.

> When we talk about creativity, we mean processes that are mean-ingful, first and foremost, for the one creating. For this reason, we do not focus exclusively on processes that are useful or valuable to society, history, or culture broadly. When a child picks up a broom-stick and playfully transforms it into a horse, that child is responding to the familiar, internalized meanings in her environ-ment, and adding a new and personal meaning to them. In practic-ing this everyday process, children develop the skills necessary to participate in processes that will ultimately be meaningful for the world as well, and the skills needed to be engaged, lifelong learners.[31]

The meaning of flying on a broomstick for the child is hardly "new" and hardly strictly "personal." Instead, play is mediated by broader narratives, ideologies, and identifications that are in part produced by culture industries. Who produces and reworks the cultural histories of the broomstick hobbyhorse? What is it that makes the broomstick horse meaningful to the child? How does the child get the idea of the broomstick horse? Who are children identifying with when they fashion and ride it? Which cultural significations function as what Stuart Hall calls the "preferred" (dominant) reading when the child imagines the broomstick as something else? What and who engages in cultural pedagogy to form the cultural inventory from which members of a culture draw to make meanings and construct intelligible narratives? Certainly, one of the players involved in cultural pedagogy is the world's largest toy company. After reading the above quote, I typed "LEGO broom-stick horse" into a search browser, and among the first things to come up was the LEGO Harry Potter toy set and a LEGO Harry flying on a broom. Perhaps the most prevalent image of Harry Potter is one of him with his schoolmates playing an imaginary game of quidditch on flying broomsticks. The LEGO Group actively produces meanings and points of identification in coordination with large media and entertainment conglomerates, such as Warner Brothers. The narrative of innocent and authentic creativity, spontaneous imagination, and play coming from the LEGO Foundation and their well-funded partners from academia and NGOs sounds quite different from the LEGO Group marketing director Michael McNally, who celebrated in the *New York Times* the power of LEGO movies to sell LEGOs by getting the film characters/media products inserted into children's play: "'We know that children's play reality involves mixing and matching characters and backdrops from our classic sets and our licensed properties,' Mr. McNally said. 'In that way, they can promote any of our mini figures or mini dolls to the role of hero in their own story.'"[32]

That quote was from 2014, when LEGO had just launched the first LEGO movie. Currently, LEGO Ventures has been spearheading the move of the LEGO Group into multimedia digital products, seeing education and gaming at the center of product development. LEGO Ventures invests in digital content companies with an eye on buying the successful ones.

LEGO EDUCATION

If the first major purpose in quantifying play is to establish play as a global learning standard that will pressure nations to buy LEGOs for education, the second major purpose is to expand the interlocking of LEGO toys with commercial data extraction and accumulation. LEGO Education sells numerous products like LEGO robots and science kits at all grade levels as STEAM (Science, Technology, Engineering, Arts, and Math) curriculum. Kits include Mindstorm, Spike Prime, and WeDo. These products tie in traditional plastic block sets with digital devices, and in the upper levels, they involve coding. LEGO markets these products for home consumption, home schooling, and school with the slogan "Rebuild the World." The advertising copy for robotic STEAM toys (that range in price from about $200 to $1,000) reads:

> Meet Hannah. Hannah is like many students who enjoy learning through play—they never see something that is beyond repair. If something breaks, they know they can always rebuild it. This is the kind of self-confidence, perseverance, and resilience that comes when engaging in purposeful play. At LEGO Education, we are committed to nurturing and growing these skills and watching students #RebuildTheWorld.

The promise of rebuilding this broken world is accomplished in the advertisements by learning to be "resilient" and "confident" by repeatedly trying to rebuild LEGO toys that break apart and fail as the child experiments with building, say, a robot. In an animated cartoon advertisement that opens the

LEGO Education website, Hannah builds a robot that gives her dog a biscuit and grows up to be an adult scientist who builds a robot on another planet. The promotion employs standard techno-utopian tropes suggesting that technology and engineering will solve the worlds' problems, which are framed as technical rather than ethical or political. For example, the WeDo kit for grades 1 and 2 has a lesson about Max and Mia's science lab getting hot, and they build a cooling fan. The activity has students build a LEGO fan. They program the fan to turn at different speeds and stop being reliant on Scratch, Jr. (a pictorial coding app). "Creativity" in the lesson involves following the prescribed model building steps to make the plastic (a petroleum product) fan by assembling the premade components.

Not mentioned in the lesson about the experience of a warming environment are the deadliest social problems facing humanity and the world, including human-caused global warming and the hotter yet possibility of nuclear annihilation—consequences of the technological domination of nature. Not only does the LEGO curriculum offer nothing to comprehend what might be breaking a world that requires rebuilding (thus reinforcing the global capitalist project of growth at any cost and the ideology of consumerism). It also suggests that the work of rebuilding requires technical practical problem-solving skills that have nothing to do with social understanding. As in the LEGO Foundation's literature promoting play-based learning, the LEGO Education toys/lessons evade engagement with the forces and interests that "break the world." For example, the Spike Prime set includes a lesson "Super Cleanup," in which students build a trash grabber. The lesson purports to teach how to test the efficacy of product designs. But there is nothing in the lesson about what produces a planet awash in trash—such as, say, a global system of capitalism that requires ever greater growth of production, consumption of needless goods, and a global culture in which consumerism is the

highest value to ensure the profits of a tiny number of ruling class people. Instead, the lesson teaches that picking up
trash requires consuming expensive plastic toys and is a com-
plicated technical problem that demands technical expertise.
In this view, pedagogy solves the world's problems by providing discreet technical skills but decidedly not by providing
the intellectual tools to investigate what breaks the world,
who breaks it, and who wins and loses from the breaking. For
example, the superrich have grown significantly richer during
the COVID-19 pandemic while continuing to roll out robots
and automation that will ensure that their companies will not
need to restore the jobs lost during the crisis.

LEGO Education advertising for their products emphasizes
that resilience and persistence developed by rebuilding toys
translates to the needed technical skills for STEM careers. Hannah in the cartoon grows up to work in a lab and puts a robot
on another planet (so much for this broken planet). Creativity,
problem-solving, and meaningful learning are framed as the
acquisition of toys and following of recipes for toy-building
that parallels the prescriptive branded play of LEGO's endless array of Hollywood branded kits. The interface with apps
means that the company can collect enormous amounts of
data (commercially valuable data) from students about how
they are using the products. This raises serious questions about
student privacy, school commercialism in the digital era, data
surveillance, and the uses of the educational apps to market
LEGO's other commercial products.

In addition, LEGO Education's products promote the ideologies of technology and consumerism under a guise of neutrality. Just as in the LEGO Foundation reports, LEGO Education
products disingenuously deny the politics of teaching, learning, and curriculum while then claiming that the depoliticized
pedagogy will form the basis of some indeterminate future
salvational activity, because technical—not social or self-
interpretative—skills will solve the world's problems. Agentic

learning involves learning to develop the intellectual tools to interpret, act on, and shape the world. To rebuild the world requires first understanding the world. However, LEGO Education promotes forms of agency at odds with learning the tools for social interpretation. Lessons are restricted to practical manipulation of and experimentation with direct experience and what exists in the present. This gives a sense of agency in which experience cannot comprehend the social forces, antagonisms, structures, and systems that produce individuals' lived experiences. Agency in the world of LEGO Education then becomes one bounded by consumer choice and empiricism. If LEGO Foundation is successful with the OECD in getting play-based learning established as a quantifiable measure of academic achievement, agency will become a quantifiably measured form of play in which imagination is restricted to a repetition of immediate reality, and creativity predominantly involves following instructions.

5 CONSPIRACY AGAINST THEORY: THE EDUCATIONAL CONDITIONS FOR RAMPANT CONSPIRACY THEORIES

Vaxxers, chemtrails, climate change hoax, birtherism, QAnon, Pizzagate, Deep State, 9/11, Holocaust denial, immigrant replacement, involuntary celibacy conspiracy theory (Incel), war against Islam, creeping Sharia. Conspiracy theories are everywhere. Their adherents are making headlines with mass shootings and are determining elections with the support of reactionary populist politicians. According to a Cambridge University 6-year international empirical study, "conspiracy theories are, nowadays, mainstream rather than marginal beliefs."[1] New and longstanding scholarship on conspiracy theories offers insights into the resurgence of white supremacy, anti-Semitism, xenophobia, and authoritarian politics and identifications.

Donald Trump typifies the extent to which conspiracy theories are now mainstream. Trump launched his political career on the birther conspiracy and ran on anti-immigrant racial and religious replacement conspiracy—Latin Americans and Muslims are replacing white Christians from the nation. Trump propelled previously fringe conspiracy theorists, such as Alex Jones, into the mainstream and has propounded conspiracy theories in which he is the principle victim: a deep state witch hunt of his presidency, and mainstream news conspiring to lie to the public with "fake news."

According to Richard J. Evans of the Conspiracy and Democracy project at Cambridge University,

> A *conspiracy theory* is an attempt to explain an event, or a series
> of events, or a phenomenon of some sort, as the outcome of a
> secret plot aiming to deprive the people illegally of money, liberty,
> power, or knowledge. . . . Conspiracy theories are a form of alter-
> native knowledge that regards knowledge produced by experts on
> events as unreliable; conspiracy theories posit an 'establishment'
> that produces 'official' knowledge, often with the ulterior motive
> of covering up the 'real truth' about something.[2]

Conspiracy theorists find in conspiracies easy answers, certain
knowledge in uncertain times, and feelings of agency. Conspiracies provide easy answers, because they come ready-made and
require neither evidence, the work of research, nor a broader
interpretive theory that can explain patterns of social phenomena. Conspiracies appear to provide certain knowledge,
because they ground proof in the persons of discreet actors.
They provide the conspiracy theorist with feelings (albeit
false feelings) of agency by offering an explanation for inexplicable and uncertain conditions. Conspiracy theories appeal
to those who experience powerlessness, and evidence suggests
that in turn, exposure to a conspiracy theory (such as view-
ing the Oliver Stone film *JFK*) results in reported increases in
political cynicism and feelings of diminished political agency.[3]

Conspiracy theories flourish in contexts of inequality and
political misrecognition. Evans claims, "More unequal countries with a lower quality of democracy tend to display higher
levels of belief in the world cabal."[4] As economic inequality and
social precarity have radically increased in the new gilded age,
political power has become concentrated, and ecological precarity looms, conspiracy theories find widespread acceptance.

Conspiracy theories tend to be less attractive to those with
higher levels of education.[5] In addition, skepticism is growing
about science, academics, journalists, and expert knowledge.
This increase is in part by design. Trump, Viktor Orban in Hun-
gary, Rodrigo Duterte in the Philippines, Jair Bolsonaro in Brazil,
Recip Tayyip Erdogan in Turkey, and other right-wing populists

who trade in conspiracy theories actively seek to erode, destroy, or co-opt knowledge-making institutions, including independent media, schools, and universities. By disseminating an abundance of lies, such populists undermine confidence in the possibility of using knowledge and education to act on and shape the social world. Epistemologically, conspiracy theories work much like Donald Trump's yellow hair and speech: ersatz, outlandish, clownish, and dubious on the surface. The real function of persistent bullshit is to undermine confidence in the capacity of individuals to obtain knowledge and to act on that knowledge, as well as to discredit knowledge-making institutions. As Jason Stanley points out, this is a standard move of fascist dictators to make the strongman's assertions the only ones that can be accepted as truth. Truth then is grounded in the body of the strongman.[6]

The commonly given reasons for the recent expansion of conspiracy theories include the proliferation of information on the internet, news provision coming from unedited social media sources such as Facebook, social insecurity, precarity, and inequality—that is, social conditions that render people powerless, so that conspiracy theories provide feelings of power and control. I suggest here that what also makes conspiracy theories particularly alluring at present involves the transformation of how knowledge and information are taught and have been taught about in both K–12 and higher education. The educational conditions for conspiracy theories have been largely absent from the public and academic discourse on the proliferation of conspiracy theories. In addition, I want to emphasize that conspiracy theories are a form of social theory (albeit bad social theory) that has to be taught and learned in place of better social theories that comprehend experience in terms of broader social forces, systems, and structures. Such better social theories provide individuals with the capacity to interpret and collectively act on public problems—conditions that are necessary for the development of a democratic society.

In what follows, I first consider the radical transformations to knowledge in education through three phases of the different capitalist uses of positivism in education. I then discuss positivism as a force propelling conspiracy theories.

THE ALIENATION OF FACT, EDUCATIONAL REFORM, AND CONSPIRACY THEORIES

Various professional and academic fields have increasingly embraced a positivist rationality in which data is said to drive inquiry and displays of numerically quantifiable progress replace efficacy. Managers, police officers, teachers, and administrators are supposed to be "data-driven." Numerous academic fields in the social sciences and humanities have eschewed theory and interpretation in favor of radical empiricism, positivism, and materialism. This trend stems in part from the expansion of instrumental and vocational commercial justifications for the remaking of fields. A few glaring examples in higher education include the ontological turns in philosophy, anthropology, and sociology; the replacement of mass communication studies with telecommunication studies; the advent of the "digital humanities" as the traditional humanities are being defunded and dismantled; and the gutting of social justice standards and educational theory from teacher and leadership preparation programs.

The neoliberalization of institutions promotes empiricism as part of an application of "scientific management" industrial efficiency models. Ever-greater efficiencies of production can only be achieved through ever-greater controls over workers and knowledge. Numerical quantification lends itself to this cult of industrial control as a commercial or exchange logic infiltrates every social space.

Yet all of this rationalization does not promote greater efficiencies, and it comes with tremendous social costs. For example, the study of knowledge disciplines (such as philosophy,

history, literature, and social and cultural theory), which are
central to societal self-reflection, are being radically reduced.
At the same time, policy has become increasingly unmoored
from rational justification and evidence for its enactment.
Some glaring examples of this include the previous US executive branch's refusal to accept the scientific consensus on
climate change, the more than 23,035 documented lies that
Donald Trump told in office as of September 2020,[7] the inten-
tional federal defunding of scientific research, and research
showing that money buys policy changes but that citizens,
movements, and evidence-based demands from the polity
have little to no impact on policies.[8] In education, there is no
evidence to support privatization schemes, such as vouchers,
chartering, and "portfolio districts" (which are just other ways
to describe privatization), yet these so-called reforms have been
promoted and implemented nonetheless. Trump's Secretary of
Education Betsy DeVos spent her career promoting voucher
schemes. Her signature achievement as Secretary of Education
was to roll back regulations on the for-profit college industry
that were in place to stop epidemic fraud (including the fraud
practiced by Trump University). The Biden administration
has admirably broken with prior Republican and Democratic
administrations' promotion of privatization unsupported
by evidence. However, it refused to allow states to suspend
standardized testing during the COVID-19 pandemic. And it
appears to have done an about face on campaign promises
to break with the decades-long excessive standardized testing of the standards and accountability movement that has
benefited test and textbook publishers but has dubious educational value and produces copious amounts of dubious data.[9]
On one hand, everything must be data driven, and on the
other hand, information, evidence, argument, and particularly
theory have little place in policy. These seemingly contradictory trends with regard to facts coalesce around what Theodor
Adorno described in his criticism of positivism.[10]

In the ideology of positivism, truth appears as a collection of facts. Facts, in this view, appear as objects without history. Facts appear to become meaningful on their own, without theoretical assumptions or interpretations. Facts appear at once ungrounded and at the same time all powerful. Fact decreasingly depends on reasoned argument or evidence and increasingly depends on assertion and hence the social authority of the speaker. Positivism is an ideology about truth claims that delinks facts from the conditions of their making and interpretation. The ideology of positivism is built into daily life and institutions, such as: the guise of disinterested objectivity in journalism that obscures the social positions and ideologies of journalists and the companies that hire them while effacing the values, assumptions, and ideologies that inform reporting; Compstat, which quantifies police work and transforms policing into boosting the numbers rather than improving community engagement; standardized testing in schools, which falsely claims as universal and neutral the partial, class, and culturally based truth claims that appear on tests and treats the results of test outcomes as learning.

As discussed in prior chapters, Adorno suggests that the allure of positivism derives from the false promise of concreteness, certainty, and solidity of numbers in a world of exchange in which everything is made abstract by being rendered into its exchange value.[11] Adorno also comprehends the logic of positivism and this promise of control as an expression of the tendency of Enlightenment rationality toward conquest—the mastery and domination of nature and the inclination to eradicate differences.[12] I would add to Adorno's observations that positivism and the allure of the seeming solidity and certainty of numbers is a response as well to the experience of a world made abstract by ubiquitous screens and the expansion of what Hubert Dreyfuss called "disembodied telepresence" that replaces bodies with digital representations, erodes one's sense of corporeal agency, and shears away social context for social exchange.[13]

Schooling produces and promotes particular conceptions of knowledge. In addition, it is a site of cultural struggle. Positivism as an ideology that delinks knowledge from its conditions of production falls on a side of cultural struggle that is hostile to theory, interpretation, judgment, and comprehension of how truth claims relate to social authority and material and symbolic interests. Positivism instead most often aligns with dogma and increasingly with market fundamentalism dressed as progress and irrationalism posing as reason.

THREE PHASES OF THE CAPITALIST USE OF POSITIVISM

There have been three modern phases when positivist rationality has been interwoven with capitalist schooling: the industrial scientific management phase, the postindustrial neoliberal privatization/accountability phase, and the new data/body privatization phase.

Throughout most of the twentieth century, schooling was refashioned based on industrial efficiency models. Scientific management developed by Frederick Taylor sought to break down the tasks of teachers and students, to routinize them, and to measure them for ever greater control and efficiency. Taylorism was imported into public schooling in the early twentieth century, and it expanded greatly during the postwar industrial era. Critical education scholars describe how the time and space of school were largely organized for social and cultural reproduction: teaching skills and know-how in forms ideologically compatible with prescribed economic roles for different classes of students. Schooling in the Fordist era created the exploitable workforce by investing long term in knowledge, skills, and dispositions compatible with the making of workers whose time and labor power could be shortchanged for owner profit. Most significantly, schools taught working class children obedience to the authority of the boss—the assumption that knowledge is grounded by authority rather than by argument. Professional class students learned different skills and ideologically bounded dispositions of dialogue, debate, and dissent that would aid them in taking leadership roles in the public and private sectors.

Positivist rationality played a central role in concealing the hidden curriculum of Fordist schooling—that is, the ways that a capitalist basis for education was obscured by tropes of merit and talent through seemingly disinterested, universally valuable, and allegedly objective mechanisms, such as testing and grades. Positivist ideology obscured and concealed the values, assumptions, and interests of those claiming official knowledge in the form of the curriculum. For example, testing and grades naturalized and depoliticized the unequal distribution of life chances by making the production of inequality appear to be the result of neutral disinterested mechanisms. Positivism also played a key role in shutting down a recognition by teachers and students of the cultural politics of knowledge and curriculum by misrepresenting truth claims as beyond contestation, conflict, and interpretation. Liberal and conservative critics of standardized testing typically at most sought to root out test bias, affirming the guise of disinterested objectivity rather than recognizing the inherently political nature of the curriculum, and making such antagonism over the curriculum the basis for linking learning to material and symbolic contests. Positivism was instrumental in deterring progressive and critical traditions of education that connect learning and knowledge to the experiences of students and the social world and that highlight relationships between truth claims and authority.[14]

From the late 1980s to the present, the neoliberal restructuring of public education, paired with the standards and accountability movement, utilized positivist ideology in a revised fashion. Neoliberal education represents another form of social and cultural reproduction in the postindustrial era. With working class industrial jobs increasingly offshored and a growing segment of the population rendered marginal to the economy, schools, particularly in working class and poor communities, moved away from reproducing the labor force through time and labor-intensive preparation for work. Increasingly, profits could be made for capitalists through short-term strategies of commodifying students and schools. As in for-profit prisons, bodies in seats became the new means of profiting through contracting. Profit-taking schemes include privatizing public schools. Giant educational management organizations win contracts to cut overhead and inflate profits; bust unions to drive down teacher pay and drive up management income; contract out, mass produce, standardize, and homogenize corporate curriculum products; and replace teacher labor with technology products. By the 1990s, the ideology of corporate culture became open and dominant, rendering the hidden curriculum overt. That is, a capitalist basis for schooling itself became dominant. In the post-Fordist era, positivism became paired with extensive and frequent standardized testing and standardized curriculum as a multibillion-dollar business itself (e.g., McGraw-Hill, Pearson, Houghton Mifflin, ETS, and Kaplan). Test failure was used by neoliberals as a justification for turning schools into businesses in the form of charters, private voucher schools, and a bevy of corporate reform schemes.

Post-Fordist schooling continued to be characterized by disciplinary power, learned self-regulation, but also by what Gilles Deleuze characterized as "societies of control." Often the imperatives for learned self-regulation (as opposed to direct corporeal control) follow a class-based pattern in the post-Fordist era. Working class and poor students have been subject to ever-greater repression and direct control as their use for generating capital decreasingly involves learned self-regulation for the labor force. They are increasingly positioned as commodified objects justifying contracting schemes in an increasingly commercialized educational system that merges with the for-profit communications and media sectors. In contrast, professional class students continue to be disciplined entrepreneurial subjects of learned self-regulation, who aim to self-manage the body, the brain, and affect. They learn that they need to manage their own bodies for competitive advantage with nootropic drugs, such as amphetamines, anxiety-control drugs, and antidepressants—all to win on positivist testing regimens that ultimately can be exchanged for economic opportunity. Technologies of direct physical control include not just the modeling of schools on the prison and military models but also massive overdiagnosis and prescription of attention deficit hyperactivity disorder (ADHD) amphetamines and antianxiety drugs, behaviorist grit pedagogies, and increasing employment of biometric pedagogical apparatus.

Positivist testing and declarations of educational failure grounded on test outcomes are used to justify these corporeal controls. The exponential increase in ADHD prescriptions for children coincided with the advent of high stakes standardized tests as teachers and parents began drugging kids to game the tests and increase the chance of ongoing school funding or to drug the kids out of distracting other test takers. Grit pedagogy, a neoliberal form of character education, employs behaviorist strategies of conditioned response to teach in ways that avoid reflection and dialogue. Biometric pedagogies use real time webcams to measure the faces of students and translate bodily movement into claims about student attention, interest, and alleged learning. Biometric pedagogy claims to measure and translate body movement into student learning and teacher performance. Pharma and media technologies make learning into a material impact on the body, evacuating mediation, thinking, critical consciousness, and knowledge production through dialogic exchange. Similarly, learning analytics, pay for success, and grit pedagogies all merge corporeal control with surveillance and measurement of bodies. Scripted lessons, a kind of quasi-religious practice of indoctrinating dogma, have continued to expand for teachers. They are now ubiquitously imposed under the guise of accountability and standards, with the resultant profits flowing to the large publishing companies. What is significant is that dialogue between teachers and students, the relationship between student subjectivity and social context, and consciousness play no part in this concept of learning. Learning is what is done to a body. Data gleaned from surveillance of bodies appears to seamlessly translate to control and measurement of both student learning and teaching as a scripted performance.

We are entering a new phase of the uses of positivism for capitalism through education that builds on the neoliberal/accountability phase and its fever for direct corporeal control. Corporeal control through direct coercion and surveillance are coming together with the making of youth into commodified data and investment securities. I observed the emergence of this phenomenon of making youth into investment securities joining with corporal security close to 20 years ago, but it is now developing through data science and learning analytics, social media, and impact investing schemes.

A few key reforms are converging that typify the data/body privatization phase: pay for success/Social Impact Bonds (as I discussed in chapter 2), adaptive learning technologies, and social and emotional learning. This convergence is justified on the basis that measurement provides accountability, and the public will not have to pay if the metrics do not show success. But even if the service is successful according to the metrics, then the public pays much more (in some cases double) for a service it could have financed directly. Schooling, reduction of juvenile justice recidivism, and child care are some of the services targeted for pay for success. Banks aim to influence the selection of programs and the evaluation. This public skimming scheme is sold under the guise of innovation, cost savings, and accountability. The privatization of the service is made into an investment bond that can be securitized by an investment bank. Increasingly, the surveillance of clients is done through data technology. In pay-for-success positivism, privatization, surveillance, and corporeal control merge as quantitative measurement becomes the justification for the value of a public project.

Another scheme of the data/body privatization phase, adaptive learning technology (discussed in chapter 2 and 3), which is promoted as a part of the personalized learning movement, has been referred to as the "Netflixing of education."[15] In this scheme, teachers are positioned as facilitators and curriculum software on screens as the teacher. Students choose lessons based on interest and test performance. Adaptive learning technology is a kind of new techno-tracking, in which a case for the student is built over time out of data collected by the students' use of the software.[16] The numbers then falsely appear as neutral, disinterested, and objective records of the students and their performance. Adaptive learning technology builds standardized testing into lessons, deepening and expanding the legacy of excessive testing and teaching to the test. Teaching and test preparation merge. Proponents of these schemes commonly claim that such technologies are "personalized," because students can move at speeds that they set for themselves. However, under the guise of personal student choice, the subjective experiences and the specific context are utterly disregarded, as is the relationship between knowledge, experience, and the social world. Thus adaptive learning technology represents a deepening and expansion of the positivism that has defined the era of test-based accountability. What is also new about adaptive learning technology and pay for success is that the capture and commodification of student data are becoming the basis for corporate profit. Adaptive learning technology projects, such as the Chan Zuckerberg

Initiative's Summit is being widely implemented in schools without a fee. But Summit, which is financially interwoven with Facebook and other for-profit education companies, is able to take student data and use it for other educational projects. The Chan Zuckerberg Initiative's other educational projects include pay-for-fee services as well as advertising-driven platforms with profit models like Facebook's. These trends are converging. Pay-for-success profiteers are moving to use adaptive learning technologies to measure and justify further pay-for-success projects.

The data/body privatization phase includes social and emotional learning schemes, such as the teaching of grit pedagogy, which are promoted through the Every Student Succeeds Act. These projects aim to make resilient individual subjects who can withstand the disinvestment in schools and communities as well as the poverty and ill effects caused by it. For example, grit pedagogy is a kind of neoliberal character education in the age of austerity that has been popularized in privatized charter schools. Like biometric pedagogy, it aims to replace learning through dialogue and student questioning and thinking with automatic response to rapid-fire scripted teacher lessons. Grit emphasizes physical control and measurement of that control as a means of learning. Learning in this view does not involve dissent, dialogue, questioning, and curiosity but learned dispositions for obedience to authority. There is an industry based on selling grit pedagogy, and grit has been promoted through privatization of schools.

The data/body privatization phase allows media corporations to hijack decisions about pedagogy and curriculum from teachers and communities, a hollowing out of the nation-state's sovereignty over one of the last large-scale public institutions. Positivism allows the values and ideologies of corporations to be concealed under the guise of disinterested objectivity and neutrality, numerical quantification, and the ideology of technological innovation, with an alibi of accountability.

CONSPIRACY THEORIES

What do the latest uses of positivist ideology have to do with the proliferation of conspiracy theories? Each phase of schooling that I have outlined has contributed to the development of an approach to knowledge that has created the conditions for conspiracy theories to flourish. Positivist standardized testing promotes *equating knowledge with authority*. In its neoliberal and data/body phases, positivism is also used to justify an approach to knowledge characterized by dogma and faith, particularly in markets. In place of dialogue, argument, and evidence, positivism erases the conditions of production for truth claims; it also disappears the actual people who make the tests and curriculum and the relationship between their social locations and their claims to truth. As Adorno pointed out, positivism locates the concept in the subject rather than in the dialectical relationship between the subject and society.[17] Positivism appeals to people, because it seems to offer certainty and foundations for truth by means of the apparent concreteness of numbers. The neoliberal and data/body phases of positivism increasingly locate truth in the bodies of students and teachers. Yet the latest uses of positivism render these subjects ever more ephemeral and fleeting as data and abstract investment securities. The student and teacher further melt into air as they are abstracted and emptied of social and educational purpose. They are transformed into data production engines tasked with generating data that has no immediate meaning but do have immediate market value, data valued for its future potential commercial worth to be realized in big data algorithms.

Enter conspiracy theories, appearing to recover the mystified social origins of facts accomplished by positivism in a particularly compelling way: by locating the origins of facts in the concrete bodies of agents. Karl Popper, who is credited with first naming the concept of conspiracy theory, described the

religious character of it. Conspirators have a mystical omnip-
otent agency.[18] In contrast to the superagents of conspiracy
theories, regular people have no agency at all. Conspiracy theories locate inflated agency/total agency in two figures: gods
and devils. Gods take form of salvational "superagents," such
as Strongmen who embody truth through aggressive assertion.
The devils—conspiratorial "secret agents" (Muslims, Jews,
blacks, women, deep state puppet masters, and so on) corporeally ground the truth and the threat of precarious social
order. Strongmen aim to make themselves the embodiment of
security, promising to protect the people whom they allege are
threatened by vilified others—the conspiratorial secret agents
who themselves are positioned as having total agency and
being existential threats to the order. Trump put it succinctly:
"Only I can protect you."

The conspiracy theory of replacement suggests that Muslims, Jews, blacks (through miscegenation, interracial marriage,
and integration), and Latin American and Asian immigrants
are conspiring to replace white Christians in the nation-state.
The replacement alleged is a physical displacement. In this
narrative, the beleaguered masses are defined by their racial
essence—the fear expressed is one of "white genocide." The
conspiratorial secret agents are also defined by their racial
essence grounded in the body—marchers in Charlottesville,
Virginia, in the summer of 2017 chanted "Jews will not replace
us"; Trump advocates a Muslim ban; the "caravans" of central
American refugees are deemed a threat. The Squirrel Hill Pittsburgh synagogue shooting of 2018 clearly expressed the logic:
Jews were conspiring to help Muslim refugees enter the nation
and the response was a sudden, violent "superhero" act of
physical annihilation of the secret agents of the replacement
threat. Similarly, Incel, which expresses male fears of being
replaced by other men and rejected by women, locates the
threat to men in the bodies of women who are framed as har-
pies or seductive destroyers, and the danger takes form in the

material fabric of their pernicious yoga pants. The Incel boys do not lobby Congress to outlaw yoga pants, develop educational projects to end women's suffrage, and so forth. Instead they idealize and emulate their superman Incel heroes who murder women in mass shootings. The men's alienation, misery, and feelings of rejection are comprehended as an effect of the women's bodies. Deep State conspirators, who are invisible bodies, seem to always target the bodies of their victims. For believers in the 9/11 conspiracy or chemtrails and for vaxxers, the mystified social origins of facts are located in their alleged physical effects.

Believers in conspiracy theories view the social as largely static and consensually formed, with the exception of the changes accomplished by superagents and the changes threatened by secret agents. Thus, conspiracy theories largely fail to recognize the multiple contests of classes and cultural groups and their symbolic and material interests, instead focusing on the perceived (and typically misrepresented) interests of a small number of historically vilified groups. Conspiracy theories typically invert power relations when it comes to these vilified groups, ascribing to them exceptional power and agency. Conspiracy theories displace social theory capable of providing a full picture of the workings of the social order by evacuating the dialectical relationship between social structure and subjectivity with a view dominated by mystified agency.

By grounding truth in the body, these theories offer explanatory power, in which alleged material essence stands in for theory, evidence, and argument. In contrast what Adorno termed "the essential" is precisely what is evacuated by positivism. Adorno writes, "the objective laws governing the movement of society which decide the fate of human beings, are essential. These laws are human destiny—though a destiny, of course, which is to be changed."[19] Both positivism and conspiracy theories obscure what Adorno terms the essential, not just the principle of exchange but also the broader social tendencies like the social antagonisms of classes and cultural groups. Positivism replaces the essential with numbers. Conspiracy theories replace what Adorno terms "the essential" with bodies who have mystified and inflated agency.

The antidote for a conspiracy theory is not merely more or better facts. Instead, the antidote is the ruthless interrogation of the social assumptions, values, interests, and ideologies undergirding claims to truth. As Adorno said, facts are always social facts.[20] Conspiracy theories deprive people of agency, because they undermine the capacity of knowledge for social agency. These theories do so by locating social agency and social change in the essentialized "facts" of groups of people rather than recognizing the material and symbolic power struggles among groups and classes. Conspiracy theories are against theory itself. Theory is a crucial tool to make experience, knowledge, and the social world objects of critical analysis. The educational task to dismantle conspiracy theories involves a project of evacuating positivism from educational practices and institutions and replacing it with a culture of education that makes central the politics of culture and knowledge.

6 TRUST IN NUMBERS, DISTRUST OF EXPERTS: EDUCATION, NEW TECHNOLOGY, AND THE PARANOID POLITICS OF DISINTERESTED OBJECTIVITY

Expertise is increasingly seen as suspect, particularly on the political right, because experts are presumed to have interests and agendas. The majority of registered Republican voters believe that higher education is "bad for America";[1] only 27 percent of Republicans trust scientists, and only 31 percent trust medical science.[2] As of this writing, most Republican voters believe that the 2020 presidential election was fraudulent and stolen, despite evidence provided by policy experts; academic experts; and thorough investigations, recounts, and audits by Republican officials at the state and local levels. In May 2021, the Republican party purged its congressional leadership for refusing to accept the stolen election lie. As of late March 2021, a quarter of Republican voters believed in the fantastical QAnon conspiracy (which includes evidence-free allegations of baby-eating Democrats running vast pedophilia rings), and this major US political party has become beholden to Trumpism with or without Trump. The 2019 book *QAnon: An Invitation to the Great Awakening by WWG1WGA* (Where We Go One We Go All) was a top 75 bestselling book on Amazon.com and included these allegations: "'that prominent Democrats murder and eat children' and that the US government 'created AIDS, polio, Lyme disease, some natural disasters, two Indiana Jones movies and the Pixar movie *Monsters Inc.*'"[3] The majority of Republican congresspeople (52 percent in the House and 60 percent in the Senate as of the 117th Congress)[4] reject the scientific consensus on global warming. Established scientific advice from public health officials to wear masks and keep a distance during the COVID-19 pandemic was rejected by rightist politicians as an infringement on individual and commercial liberty. And the scientists and public health officials are accused of political partisanship and of being commercially interested.

This chapter argues that contemporary crises of hegemony, material and symbolic precarity, and agency have fostered rising distrust of experts and specialists. An expanding distrust of experts and specialists opens questions about the relationship between knowledge and interests and calls into question the longstanding political uses of the guise of disinterested objectivity in public life. I argue that people can be educated into very different interpretations of surfacing doubts about expert knowledge and the interests behind it: a reactionary politics of paranoia, a liberal doubling down on the guise of disinterested objectivity, or critical consciousness and political agency. The first section of this chapter addresses the crises that are calling into question the guise of disinterested objectivity. The second section contends that the politics of paranoia can only take hold if it has been taught and learned. I identify three dominant tropes through which doubts about disinterested objectivity are translated into paranoia, and I detail three ways that paranoid modes of interpretation depoliticize politics, rendering collective democratic action difficult or even impossible to conceive or enact. The third section runs these issues through the recent expansion of some contemporary educational technology producers discussed in prior chapters that rely on the guise of disinterested objectivity to further commercial ends and yet build the elements of paranoid politics and pedagogy into their products. I return to the example discussed in chapters 3 and 4 of the Organisation of Economic Co-operation and Development's (OECD) discursive production of an allegedly disinterested and objective science of social and emotional learning and a problematically depoliticized criticism of it. The chapter's conclusion calls for critical pedagogical projects that can translate doubt about disinterested objectivity into critical consciousness and radically democratic politics while avoiding the alluring promise of total security with its authoritarian guarantees.

In his 1995 book, *Trust in Numbers: The Pursuit of Objectivity in Science and Public Life,* science historian Theodore Porter attempts to account for the prestige and power of numbers. Porter argues that forms of quantification are "strategies of communication" that are "intimately bound up with forms of community."[5] The reliance by public officials on numbers produced by experts, for Porter, reduces the need for "intimate knowledge and personal trust." The authority of scientific or quasi-scientific pronouncements in public life depends on claims to objectivity and the exclusion of subjectivity and judgment.[6] The appeal of numbers in policy and politics derives from faith in objectivity as being more democratic, because it is allegedly impartial, fair, and impersonal.[7] Such a view presumes that bureaucracy appeals to citizens as democratic for its guise of disinterested objectivity. As Porter points out, when public officials make decisions by referring to numbers, this not only provides an aura of disinterestedness but it also conceals the decision being made. Invoking Foucault, Porter argues that the public use of numbers conceals the politics at play and the power being wielded.[8] Yet, the allure of numbers for Porter is that they are rule-bound or officially sanctioned.[9] In public affairs, alleges Porter, "expertise has more and more become inseparable from objectivity."[10]

This assumption that expertise is inseparable from objectivity no longer holds.

Vaccine conspiracism has flourished in the present-day climate of paranoid politics. Public health experts, billionaire philanthrocapitalists, government health bureaucrats, and surpranational organizations and corporations are alleged to be conspiring to build, through the Great Reset Conspiracy, a vast biocontrol surveillance system to integrate corporate state control over the body involving the implantation of nanobot devices and bio passports sometimes said to be coordinated with 5G cell phone signals (which themselves sometimes are alleged to have caused COVID-19) under the pretext of pandemic vaccination to collect biodata and remotely control bodies. Such paranoid fantasies of conspiracy are largely produced on the political right.[11] However, even in liberal discourse, conspiracy plays a pronounced and growing role. For example, Alex Gibney's informationally rich investigative documentary *Crime of the Century* (2021) explains the opioid epidemic with its half a million deaths primarily as an *exceptional* criminal conspiracy by pharmaceutical companies abetted by corrupt politicians and doctors, rather than as a symptom of the extent to which capitalism *routinely* undermines democracy and the public interest. They do so in a systematic way by prioritizing profit for human institutions, rolling back regulatory protections, fostering the culture of predation that the film illustrates, and producing the physical and psychological damage, pain, and alienation to which narcotics addiction responds. The film frames the opioid crisis as one in a series of exceptional destructive episodes in the history of the drug business rather than as one example of capitalist pillage.[12] In this framing, medical and legal specialists are corrupted by aberrant greed from their normally disinterested and objective roles as purveyors of health and justice rather than occupying professional positions that are contested institutional terrain shot through with power relations and politics.

The politics of paranoia begins with healthy epistemic doubt and skepticism about the objectivity, disinterestedness, and neutrality of claims to truth. The trust in specialists and numbers under the guise of disinterested objectivity described by Porter in the 1990s failed to account for the nexus of corporate state interests, the role of capitalist profit seeking, and capitalist ideology in shaping and defining knowledge-making institutions. Various factors have driven such healthy skepticism about the guise of disinterested objectivity of specialists and experts, including economic precarity and hegemonic crises: the increasingly dubious legitimacy of the economic, political, and cultural social order.[13] In addition, the means of addressing these crises (that is, the tools for agency, such as education, policy influence, and journalism) have largely failed to provide citizens with the knowledge and dispositions to theorize, investigate, interpret, and judge claims to truth.[14]

For example, the means of citizens effecting change through influencing policy and legislation have been radically diminished, because nearly all legislation is enacted through purchased lobbying by the rich.[15] Education remains under the sway of positivist standardized testing and the guise of disinterested objectivity in curriculum that delinks learning from its social import and capacities for agency.[16] Schooling largely lacks critical literacies that would encourage students to interpret claims to truth in terms of the social locations of the claimant and broader structures of cultural, political, and economic power informing the context for learning. Instead, neoliberal restructuring in education has framed knowledge as something to be transmitted and consumed, rendering it into a quantifiable commodity or currency for academic and possibly later economic exchange.

Neoliberalism has displaced dialogic forms of knowledge cocreation with monologic modes of knowledge deposition. That is, it has framed knowledge as not only a commodity but also as true, legitimate, worthwhile, and beyond question, despite being written and sold by unseen authorities (such as corporate curriculum designers, and test, textbook, and tech corporations). The ascendence of standardized testing, teaching to the test, and the reduction of teaching and learning to instrumentalized skills since 2000 has transformed approaches to knowledge in public schools. The neoliberal standards and accountability movement that went hand in hand with privatization schemes positioned dialogue, debate, dissent, interpretation, judgment, and other intellectual and democratic dispositions as a liability and threat to the delivery, consumption, and enforcement of the "right" knowledge.[17]

The positivist guise of disinterested objectivity and the sanctification of knowledge through quantification belies the equating of truth with social authority. Truth appears to derive from those with power. While the assault on thinking cannot be reduced to schooling alone, the equating of truth with authority has been part of the broader educational conditions for a major portion of the US population to disregard and distrust scientists about COVID-19 masking and vaccines and to instead trust Donald Trump, even as he uttered ludicrous statements (such as suggesting injecting bleach to kill the virus). Journalism also clings to the guise of disinterested objectivity and has been recently overrun with public relations content and corporate mergers that have gutted investigative journalism.[18] Such views of science and public health expertise as being partisan and interested represents, as well, the triumph of neoliberalism's evacuation of the very concept of the public good from public discourse. In this view, all facts are considered to be merely the positions of competitive interested parties.

These economic, political, cultural, educational, journalistic, and agentic crises are part of a crisis of system legitimacy.[19] Paranoid politics and paranoid culture express material crises and symbolic crises—particularly a crisis of hegemonic legitimacy and the erosion of the institutional and cultural means for agency. For those facing precarious conditions and the widespread perception of the evaporating means to act on and shape life conditions and respond to these crises, enemies appear everywhere and anywhere. Precarity and system legitimacy in crisis raise questions and suspicions about the legitimacy of truth claims from the traditional knowledge-making institutions and experts. Such suspicions about the interests behind experts' claims call into question the guise of disinterested objectivity, the concealment of political decision, and the subjective exclusions that are wrapped up with power relations. There are different directions such doubt can take. One direction would be toward educating for critical consciousness. This would entail expanding questions about the relationships between claims to truth and forms of social authority of the claimant. Healthy doubt also involves contextualizing claims to truth in relation to the broader social, political, economic, and cultural forces, systems, and structures informing truth claims. Educating for critical consciousness fosters comprehension of the social and pedagogical formation of the self, and learning theory as "a resource that enables us to both define and respond to problems as they emerge in particular contexts."[20] As with science, we get closer to objectivity by accounting for the interests at play in the formation of truth. The politics of paranoia educates people in decidedly different directions than toward critical consciousness. It translates peoples' doubts and suspicions into fear and hatred of essentialized groups, particularly races and genders but also political parties and movements. For example, this translation appears in the right-wing media attacks on critical race theory in schools, particularly in the summer of 2021. Streaming banner headlines and vapid punditry invoke critical race theory less as a theory, argument, or lens for social analysis of structural inequality that demands remedy. Instead, right-wing news represents it more as a perjorative, a threat of black invasion of white space, and as a threat to "good schooling" that is supposed to be disinterested, apolitical, devoid of engagement with race and racism, and affirmative of existing social realities. The political spectacle of critical race theory wrapped reactionary and white supremacist cultural politics in a guise of disinterested objectivity. A central dimension of this news content was an effort to conflate a structural analysis deemed radical or Marxist with liberal multicultural efforts for diversity. According to critical race theorist Kendall Thomas, right wing activists "want people to associate critical race theory with a whole range of things that have nothing to do with critical race theory. It's a cynical effort to weaponize the illiteracy and the lack of knowledge in this country generally about race, racism and the law."[21] The sheer number of allusions to critical race theory on Fox News approached a thousand in June and nearly a thousand in July; on the right wing Newsmax station, critical race theory was mentioned 930 times. Incessant invocation of the term and paranoid, racist fearmongering stood in for arguments, discussion, dialogue, and genuine debate.

THE PEDAGOGY OF PARANOID POLITICS

A healthy skepticism toward blind faith in objectivist expert knowledge should stave off both dogmatic claims derived from radical subjectivism (in which subjective assertion delinked from argument, evidence, and theory is alleged to ground truth) and from dogmatic reference to sacred texts. Such skepticism wards off varieties of objectivism, such as positivism (claims to truth that conceal the subjective role in making it—assuming a world of facts that comes from beyond the social). As the Frankfurt School advocated, there is good reason for a distrust of excessive specialization, because such an understanding of specialization delinks knowledge from the social totality and excessively narrows understanding and the capacity for social intervention. Excessive disciplinary specialization in the humanities and social sciences has a conservatizing tendency to obscure the social and political implications of interpretation. In science and engineering, such overspecialization can result in technocratic rationality in which the social good is eclipsed by technical problem-solving or mathematical manipulation.

And yet, rejection of specialization and expertise often in the name of commercial, instrumental, practicalist ends (as Hofstadter pointed out)[22] can yield idiocy or worse. Who really wants to undergo spine surgery by a nonexpert or wants the educational system to be redesigned by businesspeople who know nothing about education or any other discipline of study? However, suspicion about expert knowledge and the interests tied to it is not widely becoming the basis for critical modes of interpretation grounded in research, theoretical investigation, and reflection about these relationships. Instead, suspicion about expertise and disinterested objectivity has largely gone in a few different directions that are at odds with critical dispositions. These paranoid politics must be taught and learned. Paranoid politics deters genuinely democratic dispositions, social relationships, and identifications in the following three ways.

(1) *The relativizing of truth claims* (particularly on the right). If everybody's claims are interested and motivated, then all claims are dubious, and there is no greater veracity to the claims of scientists, researchers, and experts than to the assertions of anyone else. Such relativizing of truth claims appears, for example, in the claims of anti-vaxxers, COVID conspiracists, QAnon adherents, and the Republican party's widespread embrace of 2020 election fraud lies. In the 2000s, Karl Rove derided the "reality-based community" for failing to see that truth is what the powerful say it is. The oil industry invoked postmodern relativism to claim that because there is minor dissent from the overwhelming consensus of the scientific community about global warming, the question remains open and hence reducing the use of fossil fuels would be unsubstantiated. These examples illustrate how relativizing truth results in authority imposing truth. Since then, information on the internet and particularly the advent of social media have resulted in a web of assertions, even as the means of editorially

controlling and vetting assertions has not expanded. (Nor has the social and educational techniques for discernment of the quality of assertion.) Such venues lack editorial processes for evaluation of evidence, argument, and theoretical underpinnings. Driven by advertising and click-through profits, content is commercially incentivized to be transgressive and incendiary, relying on emotionally potent simplification. This is fertile ground for racist, misogynist, jingoistic, and xenophobic content. As Jason Stanley has argued in *How Fascism Works,* Trump's delegitimation of the means of obtaining knowledge leaves truth in the realm of the aspiring autocrat.[23] The relativizing of truth claims disregards the difference between any random utterance and the valuable dialogic institutional processes that distinguish expert knowledge (such as editorial review, scholarly peer review, research study, or vibrant debate).

(2) *The grounding of truth claims in bodies and essentialized identities,* often in ways that presume inflated agency and conspiracy. With the rejection of expertise as partisan and interested, evidence, argument, and theory are rejected in favor of truths grounded in the alleged essence of groups of people. Racial, ethnic, and gender identity is grounded in the body, not in culture and history. This is widely practiced on the right. Examples include racist scapegoating by replacement conspiracy directed against Jews, Hispanics, Blacks, and others, and Incel scapegoating of women. The Pittsburgh Tree of Life Synagogue mass shooting and the Charlottesville white supremacist marches put such thinking out in the open. In the former, Jews were alleged to be conspiring to replace white Christians with undocumented immigrants.

The flip side of assigning conspiratorial inflated agency to maligned and scapegoated groups is assigning inflated and mystical agency to elevated superman figures, such as Trump and other Strongmen figures. In both cases, the assignment of inflated agency has explanatory power in the absence of decent social theory, evidence, or argument. Influencing left as well as right rhetorics, an outgrowth of this logic is also that essentialized groups—white men as much as others—are blamed for inequalities rather than white supremacist ideology that must be learned and can be challenged and unlearned. Such a move of conflating identity with ideology leaves white men no recourse other than guilt or defensiveness and paints antiracist forms of white identity as impossible.

(3) *Faith in data, quantification, and an uncritical perspective on science.* Paranoid politics in this form doubles down on uncritical faith in science and on the guise of disinterested objectivity and positivist ideology—truth as "just the facts" or truth deriving from disinterested expertise. In reaction to Trumpism and antiscience conspiracy mongering, many liberals and even some leftists have emphasized the valuation of science in ways that deny, as Porter points out, that objectivity in science comes from consensus in a field.[24] Science, as faith and dogma, effaces the many other critical traditions of thought, such as pragmatism and critical theory, which presume that truth is nonfoundational, provisional, fallible, and revisable. Also ignored when science becomes dogma is what Daston refers to as "mechanical objectivity" that is never fully attainable.[25] Such automated means of generating knowledge conceal the subjective dimensions of objectivity. For example, artificial intelligence (AI) education systems have built into the design of the teaching machine implicit and seldom exposed assumptions, values, ideologies, and curriculum selections that inform without examination both the meanings produced by the use of the technology and the interpretation of the data generated by student use. Purveyors misrepresent these technologies as providing neutral, objective, disinterested, and quantifiable knowledge.

These three problematic responses to the dubiousness of disinterested objectivity and expertise need to be comprehended as both political and pedagogical. Paranoid modes of interpretation depoliticize politics by recasting the relationships between knowledge and interests. Paranoid politics diverts suspicion about the relationships between objectivity and interests away from critical theoretical dispositions and instead channels it into forms of social interpretation that evacuate politics. The politics of paranoia depoliticizes by making agonism into antagonism, depoliticizing agency, and it drives liberal reaction that doubles down on the guise of disinterested objectivity, replacing politics with a liberal consensus concern with "polarization" and "extremes."

(1) *Making agonism into antagonism.* Social and political theories of hegemony, such as radical democracy theory, presume that society is constituted by difference and contestation among competing classes and cultural groups that aspire to social ascendancy. For Chantal Mouffe, radically democratic societies can make difference and contestation central to politics.[26] She calls for an agonistic rather than antagonistic politics. Agonism overcomes the problem of liberalism's effacement of difference and power relations under the rubric of consensus. It also addresses the possibility that contestation and difference can become "antagonistic"—that is, that the political adversary is transformed into an enemy to be annihilated. Paranoid politics translates rightful suspicion about the interests tied to specialized knowledge into an antagonistic form of politics. In this form of politics, blame for economic inequality and political misrepresentation is displaced onto the victims of structures and systems and particularly on their alleged essential identities grounded in their bodies. Suspicion about the interests and ideological perspectives linked to truth claims can result in the good work of interpretation, contestation, and debate about meanings and representations—that is, engagement in cultural politics. Engagement with contested claims leads to dialogic exchange and the arrival at truth through debate, dissent, curiosity. It can also lead to the grounding of truth claims through argumentation, evidence,

the explication of the theoretical assumptions behind claims to truth, and consideration for how the social position of the participants (or location of the researcher) relates to the views being espoused (standpoint). Such a view of knowledge-making as cultural politics does not only present a more accurate picture of how culture works (as Stuart Hall shows) and how science works; it also accords with radically democratic dispositions, values, identifications, and practices.

Radical democracy as a political theory rejects the consensus-oriented politics of the liberal philosophical tradition that conceals the power interests of hegemonic groups. It also rejects the post-politics/post-ideology of neoliberalism that makes politics into a matter of managerialism and falsely presumes the end of ideological contestation. In addition, radical democracy rejects rightist authoritarian populism that seeks to make politics the will of the strongman or oligarchy. There is an affinity between the contested and dialogic forms of knowledge-making and radical democratic political theory that aims for democratic social relations. Radical democracy makes the valuation of difference and agonism central by building on Antonio Gramsci's conception of hegemony. This idea of hegemony recognizes that the social order is never once and forever fixed but rather is subject to contestation and struggle, and it depends on winning blocs by educating others into consent. However, the politics of paranoia teaches people to turn against the recognition of hegemonic agonism and turn toward what Mouffe calls "antagonistic" forms of politics, in which the adversary is seen as an enemy to be annihilated.[27] In paranoid politics, difference is positioned as threat rather than as a necessary part of the act of knowing and as constitutive of political community. Radical democracy theory sees identity formation through the process of identification accomplished by the pedagogical production of representations and subject positions. This nonessential conception of identity aims for the linkages of different identities through a common identification with the emancipatory aspirations of radical democracy—what Mouffe calls "the chain of equivalency."[28] Radical democracy's non-essential conception of identity recognizes that identity and ideological convictions do not necessarily align. The politics of paranoia frames identity as essential; draws lines around the identity-based political community; corporealizes politics; and refuses to recognize the pedagogical, deliberative, and interpretive processes of culture and politics.

(2) *Replacing political agency with depoliticized forms of agency: conspiracy, bad interpretive frameworks, mechanical objectivity in machines.* Failing to comprehend politics as the consequence of meaning-making and educative work, the politics of paranoia sees social change as the consequence of the secretive and inexplicable dealings of those with mystically inflated agency. In the politics of paranoia, conspiring agents and minoritarian groups have an inexplicable capacity to achieve social ends. The powerful have inflated agency and are worshipped for their exceptionality. Might makes right. Knowledge and learning are not seen as tools for social and political agency. Yet in the logic of paranoid politics, everything can be a potential clue to unveil conspiracy—the secret plan that determines social reality enacted by secret players with secret motives. As the first QAnon post puts it, "everything has meaning." The point not to be missed is that QAnon and other conspiracies fan the flames of conspiracy without providing a social theory or explanatory framework than can account for social change or subjective motivation. They cannot explain acts of interpretation in terms of how material and symbolic interests relate to social systems, social structures, and social patterns. Sometimes these conspiracies hang on ludicrous and flimsy motivations, such as QAnon's assertion of a vast ring of politicians and rich liberals preying sexually or cannibalistically on children.[29] But these fantastical conspiracies respond to a very real experience of contemporary electoral politics as failing to represent the values and interests of many people. Other

conspiracies claim that the 5G cell signals cause COVID-19 or that Bill Gates, Anthony Fauci, the World Health Organization (WHO), and the pharmaceutical industry are scheming to control bodies by implanting nanobots via vaccines. These conspiracies touch on the unaccountable workings of corporate power and the rightful fears of the unchecked growth of surveillance and citizen/consumer profiling and the automation of labor in data capitalism. These conspiracies mistake the structural workings of capitalism as a system and its imperatives for growth and profit at any cost with the nefarious intent of particular actors or organizations with untold power. These "bad social theories" fail to provide an account for how subjects are socially, politically, economically, and ideologically formed or how agents can learn to think and act in ways that depart from the social positions they may originate from and the ideological positions that are presumed to be aligned with those social positions. Conspiracism does not account for the development through learning of consciousness, critical or otherwise, mediation that is sometimes contradictory, negates the existing order or the imagining of better futures. It paints a picture of a world of social Darwinian opportunism, a world of sharks, in which motivation corresponds to identity and identity corresponds to interests.

(3) *Worries about "political polarization."* Democracy depends on public debate, deliberation, and dissent. Yet it is common to read interpretations of political polarization as a problem. In this view, social media "echo chambers" reinforce individual political ideological propensities, thereby pitting people against one another and driving them further apart politically. In this framing, truth and politics are recast through an unsettling deficit of consensus. What disappears when "extreme" disagreement becomes the problem are the political, economic, and ideological interests of competing social groups and classes. Coming to terms with the political means being honest about how interests and ideological perspectives

undergird claims to truth and people's positions, including those of experts. Increasingly the political right has been using a demand for K–12 and higher education to be "inclusive" of all sides of an issue (what's the other side of slavery or the holocaust?), passing legislation in Florida (HB 233) and Texas (HB 3979) among other states with Republican-dominated legislatures that is designed to allow vigilante lawsuits or sanctions against schools or universities in which professors or teachers fail to support right-wing positions. In this context, the guise of disinterested objectivity is being used to wage war on public educational institutions while promoting the inclusion of hard right ideologies and the exclusion of any examination of systemic inequality, particularly with regard to race.

THE PARANOID POLITICS OF NEW EDUCATION TECHNOLOGY

I have been arguing that crises of hegemony inform suspicions about the disinterestedness and objectivity of specialization and expertise in public life. Furthermore, suspicion about the guise of disinterested objectivity can go in the direction of criticality and democratic possibility, or it can take the direction of the politics of paranoia. This section provides several examples of how the elements of the politics of paranoia described earlier in this chapter are being spread through newly established for-profit educational technology products. The crucial task ahead is to create the educational conditions for questioning the relationships between knowledge and social authority as the basis for critical dispositions and for those critical dispositions to be the basis for collective struggle for redistributive justice, equality, and emancipation. As William I. Robinson notes in *The Global Police State*: "it must be reiterated time and again that it is capital's implacable drive to accumulate that leads it to plunder the environment, to expropriate land and resources, to waste and pillage communities everywhere, and to impose a global police state to contain the explosive contradictions of an out-of-control system . . . this all comes to the outcome of social and class struggle."[30]

This system depends on language, culture, and common sense to give it intelligibility. Education is a crucial site of and a stake in the struggle for the future. In its formal and informal settings, education produces knowledge and common sense, and it affirms or challenges broader discourses while also creating points of identification and subject positions for people to occupy. The guise of disinterested objectivity in education and the denial of the politics of education is profoundly reactionary, as it affirms the existing social order.

I want to examine an important but problematic intervention in the contemporary construction of allegedly disinterested objective educational science by experts. What is particularly problematic in the first example below is the lack of a broader normative political framing that would comprehend the production of the guise of disinterested objectivity in terms of broader material and symbolic contests and the politics of education.

Quantification of Social and Emotional Learning

As discussed in chapters 3 and 4, noted scholars of education and new technology Ben Williamson and Nelli Piattoeva have observed how the OECD has produced a discourse of scientific objectivity for a relatively new educational trope, social and emotional learning, in order to legitimate it and build it into international quantified comparisons among nations through standardized testing. Social and emotional learning is an educational discourse that, according to the Collaborative for Academic Social and Emotional Learning (CASEL), "is the process through which all young people and adults acquire and apply the knowledge, skills, and attitudes to develop healthy identities, manage emotions and achieve personal and collective goals, feel and show empathy for others, establish and maintain supportive relationships, and make responsible and caring decisions."[31]

This project aims to teach the comprehension and self-regulation of affect and emotion; to teach empathy and "healthy" relationships. Social and emotional learning was developed in part in reaction to the standards and accountability movement in education that, under the guise of disinterested objectivity, has reduced teaching to that which is testable, quantifiable, and measurable. Though social and emotional learning purports to remedy the decontextualization of knowledge, teaching, and learning, it has developed principally through psychological tropes that are depoliticized and individualistic. For example, social and emotional learning does not teach ways of comprehending experience in relation to the broader social forces that produce those experiences, nor does it teach students ways of understanding emotions and affect to be able to act on and shape the social contexts they inhabit. Williamson and Piattoeva do not address the cultural politics and implicit pedagogy of social and emotional learning but instead focus on how behavior, affect, and subjective experience are being translated into a new quantified/datafied quasi-science. This quantification of social and emotional learning is being done in conjunction with a human capital and econometrics discourse that will be used for commercial and surveillance purposes through big data psychoinformatics that can track and predict student behavior.

The Williamson and Piattoeva analysis provides valuable insights about how discursive practices construct the alleged objectivity of a field through quantification of behavior and affect. They write: "Our main claim is that SELS, as a contested science in the making, embodies attempts by policy influencers to stabilize the field through the production of objectivity, while broadening and consolidating the uses of education technology." They elaborate on how affect and behavior are standardized, how the standardized measures are made into measurement technologies, and how data production is then used to promote policy and a "marketplace for technology providers."[32]

Williamson and Piattoeva draw on Alain Desrosières and Porter to argue that quantification became "allied with objectivity not because it mirrored reality more accurately, but because numbers were easily transportable. Numbers may be shared across disciplinary divides and cultural borderlines, enabling effective communication between parties whose goals, interests and beliefs may be otherwise different" (Williamson & Piattoeva, 69). Moreover, they discuss "procedural objectivity" that "highlights the role of impersonal, standardized methods of investigation."[33] Procedural objectivity removes the "problematic" human from the pursuit of truth by measuring and standardizing data across sites, making an "independent, standardized experimental apparatus" to achieve the same results in different places.[34] The authors point out a tautological dimension to the objectivity production of science. "Standardized analytical categories are the precondition for building standardized measurement tools that help to render uniform results, thus proving the theory that underlies the endeavor in the first place."[35] So, in keeping with their example, the standardized measures of social and emotional learning that are invented evacuate the cultural specificity and contexts of their origins and makers. The standardization, measurement, and numerical quantification then provides an aura of scientific authenticity and the guise of objectivity. As Robin Truth Goodman points out, the imperative for standardization, measurement, and quantification of experience, behavior, and affect belies a paranoia about that which is uncontrollable in the human, that which cannot be turned into data and profit.[36]

Significantly, Williamson and Piattoeva criticize the ways that the field of knowledge effaces contested categories and the subjective aspects of truth formation. However, their analysis of the discursive production of objectivity does not directly address class and cultural power and the material and symbolic interests in "stabilizing the field" by producing objectivity. While they do represent discursive production in a way that specifies beneficiaries of the project of making a standardized and quantified social and emotional learning—the technology industry, supranational organizations, governments, policy actors—they *do not* specify the victims of this project or the broader structuring social antagonisms that animate these kinds of projects. That is, their analysis would benefit from being situated in a broader class and ideological analysis that sees a project such as this one as a part of hegemonic struggle. Hegemonic blocs naturalize and universalize their particular material and symbolic interests. The project of making a quasi-science out of social and emotional learning is a political economic project that involves the redistribution of governance and decision making from public schools, public school teachers, and staff to private technology corporations. This redistribution is a part of the broader privatization of public goods and services and part of the even broader neoliberal restructuring of society that has been waged by a transnational capitalist class on people of both the working and professional classes since the late 1970s.

How does this case of the OECD's project of translating social and emotional learning into quantifiable data that can form the basis for commercial extraction of children and social control relate to the politics of paranoia? This example is part of a broader pattern in which new educational technology projects fabricate a positivist quasi-science of behavior, affect, and subjectivity first under the *guise of attention to subjectivity* in order to deploy this quasi-science as objective. This social and emotional learning project, along with many others—including adaptive learning technology, biometric pedagogy projects, and the play-based learning movement—all claim to be attentive to student subjectivity, local contexts and cultures in order to promote pedagogies that utterly disregard student subjectivity, local contexts and cultures, and differences. But all these projects then set the stage to expand the guise of disinterested objectivity in quantifying and datafying affect and behavior.[37] They all aim to induce children to produce data for financial gain by use of standardized, decontextualized pedagogical technologies.[38] In fact, promoters of these various commercial educational projects appropriate progressive language and concepts such as agency and culturally relevant pedagogy. The crucial point is that this new technology trend in education enacts paranoid politics as it deters genuinely democratic dispositions, social relationships, and identifications by grounding truth in social authority; by grounding truth claims in bodies and essentialized identities; and by promoting a faith in data, quantification, and an uncritical perspective on science.

Earlier in the chapter I discussed how the neoliberal standards and accountability movement contributed to the conditions for political authoritarianism by undermining dialogic, intellectual, and critical approaches to education but also by promoting positivist approaches to knowledge, in which knowledge is legitimated by the social authority of the claimant. These new educational technologies continue, deepen, and expand these tendencies while gaining greater social legitimacy by automating and technologizing quantification. What should not be missed as well is that paranoid interpretations of the uses of these technologies misunderstand the broader structural and systemic tendencies at play, explaining these technologies as conspiracies by super-agents rather than as the development of capital through data science, AI technology, militarized accumulation, and positivist ideology.

Adaptive Learning Technology

Adaptive learning technologies (as discussed in chapters 2 and 3) have been called "the netflixing of education," because they use AI to change curriculum or change the speed of curriculum delivery in response to the student's use while building a long-term case about the student's achievement and making predictions about the user's interests or capacities.[39] Although adaptive learning companies such as the Chan Zuckerberg Initiative's (CZI) Summit promote the technology product as culturally relevant and attentive to individual students and the context, it is not. Instead, the technology largely speeds up or slows down the delivery of standardized and homogenized curriculum content. The data that students are induced to produce through their mandated use of the technology is then taken by CZI, which is a limited liability company that also owns and acquires for-profit education companies. The limited liability company's use of third-party data raises serious concerns about student privacy.[40] The data produced is a valuable commercial asset. The case being made about individual students stands to deepen a kind of "techno tracking," exacerbating the ways that social and cultural reproduction plays out through schooling. The pedagogical approach suggests that teachers are facilitators, and the real teacher is the technology. Adaptive learning technology displaces dialogic forms of teaching and learning in favor of a transmissional model of pedagogy. It undermines the capacity of teaching to address the relationship between claims to truth, the subjectivities of students, and the meaning of truth claims in a particular social context.

Avatars for Literacy and Social and Emotional Learning

New educational technology investors, such as the New Schools Venture Fund created by venture capitalist and long-time educational privatizer John Doerr, invest in for-profit start-ups, such as online curriculum companies involved in student surveillance and data tracking (Class Dojo), avatars that teach literacy through scripted lessons and phonics (Amira Learning), and gamified online curriculum products (Centervention). The data produced by students is a valuable commercial asset. The programs track, predict, and direct future behavior. The truth of the student is located in the body under surveillance. Centervention's Zoo U teaches students social and emotional learning by having them sit in front of a computer screen (instead of interacting with human beings), watch animated cartoons, and play video games about social interactions, even as the technology is incapable of engaging with the unique specificities of student subjectivity or cultural context. Amira Learning's avatar teaches students reading by having students sound out words, but it offers nothing in the way of engaging with the meaning of language or the social meaning of texts. Learning in these examples is about nothing more than the learning of discrete and decontextualized knowledge, and technical skills rather than understanding that could form the basis for social comprehension and action.

Biometric Pedagogy

The Bill & Melinda Gates Foundation, a neoliberal venture philanthropy in education, spent millions to study biometric wrist sensors to measure teachers' efficacy by their effects on the bodies of students. Similarly, Affdex developed webcam biometric facial scanners to measure teacher efficacy by the physical changes to students' faces. A Montessori school named Wildflower puts biometric tracking slippers on toddlers to accumulate and crunch movement data.[41] These products presume that learning can be read from the bodies of children. There is no place in this model of pedagogy for dialogue, thinking, mediation, or the relating of knowledge to experience and the broader social world. Truth claims are grounded in the body of students to be read off by the technology.

Play-Based Learning

LEGO Foundation and the OECD have been pushing for the quantification of play-based learning and the making of play-based learning into a quantifiable global learning standard.

LEGO, the largest toy maker in the world, is moving to the interface of traditional physical toys with online apps, data commerce, and for-profit education initiatives. The OECD is pursuing the same aims as with the social and emotional learning quantification project: facilitating social control and corporate profit. Again, truth is found in the body and is to be quantified and measured through the use of apps.

It would be all too easy to explain as conspiracies this trend of quantifying and standardizing affect and behavior into data for commerce by billionaires (such as Zuckerberg and Gates), supranational organizations (such as the OECD), corporations (such as LEGO) and these tech companies. Instead, they collectively represent the project of what William Robinson calls "militarized" capital accumulation through extraction of the lifeworld. That is, such new forms of privatization that displace teacher labor with technology and manufacture children's data respond to the crisis of surplus capital, capital's need for ever new places to invest, and the crisis of legitimacy for capitalism. These projects create new markets, in part by pillaging public education, public labor, and the lived experience of childhood. These projects also function ideologically and pedagogically to produce forms of teaching and learning that deny the politics of knowledge and the relationships between truth claims and authority; to treat learning as an effect on bodies; and to undermine forms of dialogue that can facilitate interpretation and judgment of the interplay between knowledge, self, and society.

In all these examples, paranoid politics and pedagogy is evident in terms of the antidemocratic pedagogical approaches promoted by these technologies; the approach to learning, social relations, and society taught by these technologies; and the assumptions, values, and ideologies undergirding these products. All these technologies aim for profit through ever greater control over youth. In addition, these technologies promote faith in data and truth as quantification of decontextualized fact rather than fostering modes of interpretation in which students learn to analyze the values, assumptions, ideologies, and material and symbolic contests behind the formation of data, which makes that data meaningful in a particular context. These technologies reveal a profound paranoia about the uniqueness, spontaneity, and varieties of human experience and cultures, not to mention thought and imagination that cannot be standardized, measured, and controlled.

Rising distrust of specialists and expertise driven by these crises opens questions about the politics of knowledge and interests. The political right channels doubt and distrust of expertise towards hatred, scapegoating, and authoritarianism. Alternatively, the right kinds of educational projects can foster critical pedagogies, the development of critical consciousness and democratic dispositions that comprehend the politics and power relations involved in claims to truth by experts. Contemporary crises of hegemony and agency foster scepticism about the relationship between specialization and truth. This scepticism has enabled new authoritarian modes that relativize truth and equate it with power while falsely grounding identitarian truth in essentialized bodies and reified data. However, this scepticism also challenges the guise of disinterested objectivity that denies the dialectical relationship between subjectivity and objectivity: the ways that subjects are formed pedagogically and ideologically in part through the instantiation of social antagonisms and the ways that subjects are implicated in the investigation, interpretation, and formation of contested knowledge.

The critical, political, and pedagogical task ahead is to translate the proliferating doubt about the guise of disinterested objectivity into critical modes of interpretation that can form the basis for public action. On one hand, this suggests eschewing both the total distrust of expertise now prevalent on the right and the guise of disinterested objectivity in its individualized professional forms, embracing instead the valuation of expertise as universally interested. That is, forms of specialization and expertise need to be situated in terms of human and planetary benefit rather than in terms of disinterested technical efficiency and the logic of accumulation, exchange, mastery of nature, and domination. Getting there is a political and educational project. The effort would entail fostering critical literacies and modes of investigation of the relationships between claims to truth and forms of social authority of the claimant; contextualizing claims to truth in relation to the broader social, political, economic, and cultural forces, systems, and structures informing truth claims. It also demands educating people to comprehend, criticize, and reject the politics of paranoia that translates doubts and suspicions into fear and hatred of essentialized groups, particularly races and genders but also political parties and movements. The critical pedagogical response to the politics of paranoia in its various guises has to involve grounding interpretation in broader egalitarian and emancipatory normative political and ethical referents. Critical pedagogical practices in all places where culture is produced and meanings are made can be sites for cultural criticism and cultural production. Such practices can respond to the politics of paranoia and its scapegoating, essentialism, depoliticization, and antidemocratic representations and identifications. Critical pedagogical practices can respond by producing radically democratic identifications and subject positions; educating about the systemic causes that structure selves and societies; and teaching the tools for educated interpretation, informed judgment, and democratic dialogue and exchange. A crucial task is to reject the ideologies of technology utopianism and the mistaken framing of AI and other new technologies as autonomous expressions of "mechanical objectivity"—that is, as somehow beyond interpretation, cultural politics, and cultural pedagogy.[42]

The politics of paranoia spreads a culture of distrust and framing of all as the enemy to be potentially annihilated.

Critical pedagogy can spread a culture of trust in people to use knowledge collectively for shared benefit and associated living, even as associating with others must involve recognizing their differences. Trusting others; expanding social relations of solidarity; and embracing an inherently agonistic society, self, and culture is bound up with a certain embrace of the inherent risk of living—a risk that parallels the very risk of using language and being misunderstood, because language is characterized by an ineradicable slippage in meaning at the core of signification. As social psychologist and Frankfurt School social philosopher Erich Fromm wrote in response to the specter of nuclear annihilation through Mutually Assured Destruction during the Cold War,

> Closely related to the problem of the mode of paranoid thinking is the wish for absolute security. . . . This craving is irrational (1) because there is no absolute security in life, (2) because once it is established as the dominant goal there is no limit to the means sought for the reach this goal, (3) because in the search for this goal the person cripples himself and loses all pleasure in living. In fact, the chase after security is a boomerang: It creates more insecurity than it avoids.[43]

Fromm's insight reminds us that the politics of paranoia depends on a destructive fantasy of total security that involves the impossible dream of shutting down social agonism, politics, and difference as well as the fantasy of abdicating the self to the bigger body and its promise of total incorporation—the fascist promise. Radical inequality and the precarity, hegemonic crises, and agentic and democratic crises produce disorientation and demands for security. The response to this must be to struggle for human and planetary security but within what Stuart Hall called a "politics without guarantees"[44]—a promise of vibrant and contested democratic culture with difference and agonism at the core.

7 "PRIVILEGE CHECKING," "VIRTUE SIGNALING," "AFFINITY GROUPS," AND "SAFE SPACES": WHAT HAPPENS WHEN CULTURAL POLITICS IS PRIVATIZED AND THE BODY REPLACES ARGUMENT

Previous chapters detailed how, in the face of material and symbolic precarity, crisis of hegemony, and the erosion of the traditional mechanisms for collective agency, people grasp for certainty in the concreteness of immediate fact, data, numerical quantification, and the body. This chapter focuses on how, in the face of precarity and uncertainty, certain strains of progressive thought have fallen prey to concepts that frame politics through the essentialized body, the personal, and the private domain. I contend that the allure of the false certainty of the body undermines the capacity of progressives to challenge oppression.

In this chapter, I discuss four expressions about symbolic power and social privilege that have wide usage and popularity in online media culture and everyday speech but are largely unused in scholarly academic discourse. Two of these expressions, "privilege checking" and "safe space," can be found in campus projects sponsored by student groups and offices of institutional diversity and inclusion that aim to influence campus culture. The expression "virtue signaling" refers to the act of expressing online outrage about injustice by a privileged person to other privileged people to elevate symbolic standing.

Both online and on campus, the terms "privilege checking" and "safe space" signify an effort to educate students and others into speech and behavioral practices that are intended to represent the symbolic interests of historically oppressed minorities. Although class, racial, ethnic, gender, sexual, and other forms of historical privilege are all too real, destructive, and determining of life opportunities, here I am questioning how, since the 1990s, efforts to challenge privilege have moved away from public engagement and toward private and personal forms of redress. The implications of this trend are that progressives are inadvertently fueling the opposition while undermining their capacity to forge social justice projects. For example, as white supremacy becomes increasingly public in its expressions, antiracism is taking private and individualized forms. What is at stake here is not only that the private form of antiracism is incapable of contributing to a left politics capable of defending public forms of democracy. What is also at stake is that these private forms of antiracism are inadvertently ceding public space and public discourse to white supremacist, white nationalist, xenophobic, and fascist political expressions and movements. In so doing, private forms of anti-oppressive expression redefine politics in ways that exacerbate the neoliberal evacuation of the very concept of the public and redefine culture in forms that are at odds with the public use of reason for collective benefit.[1]

The different terms ask different things of culturally subordinate and dominant individuals. Privilege checking largely asks members of historically privileged and culturally dominant groups to recognize their social advantage during dialogue with subordinate groups. At times, the injunction to "check your privilege" is less of a request for reflection or recognition of the subordinate status of minorities than a way to end the exchange. For example, a widely referred to website blog from 2006 provides a guide to checking your privilege that includes the recommendations to "learn to listen rather than speak" (Shrub.com blog). In this case, the request of the party claiming subordinate status asks that the party alleged to possess privilege withdraw from the dialogue. The logic here is that the historically oppressed person's group has been silenced, and now it is the time for the privileged person's group to be silent. The tendency of the call to "check your privilege" as a way to end the exchange and silence the alleged oppressor shuts down a political and public conception of culture as a form of dialogic (albeit unequal) exchange.

While privilege itself is a collective phenomenon pertaining to groups, the injunction to "check your privilege" positions the resistance work of cultural politics as a "clap back" done by an individual to another individual recipient of privilege.[2] The call for privilege checking differs from cultural production activity that calls for collective action to address the structures and systems that produce and affirm symbolic hierarchies. Privilege checking is an individual response to a public problem.

Often the call for privilege checking represents what Angela Nagle refers to in *Kill All Normies* as "Virtue Signaling"—a competition for moral superiority among the privileged, in which online expressions of outrage at oppression are far less intended to mobilize anti-oppressive politics than they are intended to symbolically bolster the standing of the speaker/writer.[3] Similarly, Phoebe Maltz Bovy describes the call to check your privilege as, "more typically, it's a way for someone privileged to play self-appointed spokesperson for the marginalized, so as to win a sensitivity competition with others similarly aloof."[4] Virtue signaling is an individualized strategy for symbolic dominance intended to mark the speaker's purity by targeting the speech of other progressives as insufficiently pure. The aim is to shame and silence. To be clear, I am not arguing that there is never an occasion to silence or shame. For example, Chantal Mouffe provides a conception of radically democratic political community that necessarily excludes political identities that are defined by their antidemocratic values. However, virtue signaling is a practice that erodes political community, ethical commitments, and solidarity in the interest of staging a quasi-politics of online display.

The virtue-signaling maneuver of silencing does not recognize the pedagogical dimensions of culture as a counterhegemonic practice that involves acting in a Gramscian sense as a permanent persuader to educate the opponent about the common sense of organic intellectuals. More specifically, privilege checking tends to suture privilege to identity, concealing rather than revealing the fictive nature of identity formation and undermining the pedagogical possibilities of rearticulating oppressive identity positions in anti-oppressive forms.

In the 1990s, cultural studies encouraged us to fixate on criticizing essentialized identity. Peggy McIntosh's "White Privilege: Unpacking the Invisible Knapsack" called on whites to examine their unexamined privilege. The late 1990s saw efforts to make whiteness an examined racial category rather than a neutral default nonracial identity category. In addition to McIntosh, Ruth Frankenburg, Joe Kincheloe, and Henry Giroux (1997) among others called for making white racial identity the subject of critical scrutiny.[5] The effort to center whiteness as a racial category faced colorblind discourse across the political spectrum. The right called for colorblindness and the denial of race as the solution to racism. In addition, some scholars on the left, such as David Roediger, called for the abolition of whiteness.[6] As Stuart Hall's work in the 1990s emphasized, the discourse on race is a floating signifier, a social construction, a fiction, and yet it is a fiction with real material effects. Giroux argued that colorblind discourse could not address white supremacy in its symbolic and material manifestations, and he emphasized the centrality of pedagogy to the production of race. Giroux argued for recognizing that whiteness as a racial category is pedagogically produced and can be produced in forms that are defined through antiracism. Giroux, notably in the book *Channel Surfing*, contended that left calls for abandoning whiteness affirmed broader discourses of whiteness as defined through either liberal white guilt and shame or right-wing discourses of white pride, white power, and white supremacy.[7] Giroux's argument for cultural pedagogical projects that redefine whiteness through democratic commitments to equality and justice suggested a way of collectively addressing white supremacy. Here the call is for pedagogical projects that highlight the constructedness and discursivity of race that link the identity position of racial privilege to efforts to challenge the systemic reproduction of symbolic and material privilege. In other words, Giroux was calling for people to do cultural work that produced new identifications of whiteness, forms that would be defined through antiracism linked to other struggles for equality and justice. This is precisely what needs to be done.

However, since the 1990s, identity politics discourse has largely slipped back into racial essentialism bolstered by the tendency for personalized forms of cultural politics. As Asad Haider points out, identity politics originated with a radical intersectional class and race analysis that was largely remade by neoliberal Democrats, such as the Clintons, who evacuated class politics from it and turned against the legacy of the civil rights movement.[8] The beginning of the Obama era witnessed a liberal/neoliberal affirmation of colorblind discourse, in which racial politics were persistently steered toward the personal and away from the political. The Obama White House "beer summit" with Henry Louis Gates, Jr. and Cambridge Police officer James Crowley typified the trend with the personal encounter between individuals positioned as the only form of redress. Similarly, the Trayvon Martin killing was met with Obama's statement that Martin could have been Obama's son. The impulse to personalize asks the listener to identify with and empathize with the victim of racial violence. But for a growing minority of the country, the personalization of politics fed not into empathy but dreams of violence fueled by a fear of lost personal power and displacement of whites by nonwhites, Jews, Muslims, immigrants, and foreigners. At the same time, institutional and extrajudicial white supremacist murders of Black men have become more frequent. Overt white supremacy and expressions of white pride and white nationalism have entered mainstream public discourse and political discourse along with record levels of hate incidents in the post–Civil Rights era and overt xenophobia, race-baiting political statements. In other words, white supremacist discourse has become increasingly public in its efforts at pedagogical engagement and persuasion as antiracism has embraced the private, the personal, feelings, and the body. As the overpass banners, marching slogans, and graffiti illustrate, essentialized white identity is proud and defensive, positioning not just difference as the enemy but the liberal white alignment of whiteness with guilt and shame. Liberals and white supremacists share a tendency to essentialize racial identity. During the 2021 right-wing misuse of "critical race theory" to intervene in the public-school curriculum, Fox News pundit Tucker Carlson absurdly took the going public of white supremacy a step further. He suggested that teachers wear body cameras so parents can monitor their classroom teaching for any discussion of critical race theory. The not-so-subtle suggestion was that the teaching of antiracism in public schools is a kind of violence akin to the disproportionate murder of African Americans by white police officers, who are commonly required to wear body cameras. Carlson described critical race theory as not just "BS" but "civilization-ending poison" and gave his commentary with an on-screen logo of the Democratic Party and the words "Anti-White Mania."[9] Carlson's suggestion was consistent with the growing entry into the public realm of defensive proud white supremacist action. By personalizing and essentializing racial discourse while conflating white identity with guilt and shame rather than collective forms of antiracist solidarity, liberal leaders like Robin DiAngelo[10] cede public space to white supremacists like Carlson.

Like privilege checking, the safe space makes anti-oppressive politics personal, individual, and tied to the body. The concept of the safe space distinguishes designated safe spaces that are places for oppressed minorities to talk with, be counseled by, or confide in a trained ally. Designated safe spaces, such as a faculty member's office marked with a sticker earned from a safe space training, promote a conception of the campus space generally and the classroom in particular as dangerous space. The safe space needs its constitutive outside and that outside (i.e., the rest of the campus) is, as Laura Kipnis observes, fraught with peril. The danger comes especially from speech that is alleged to make somebody feel uncomfortable or traumatized.

Like the safe space, the student "affinity group" is a growing trend in K–12 and higher education that addresses inequality and injustice through a privatized remedy of voluntary association. In place of a political movement or collective remedy in the institution that involves all students, such as incorporating anti-oppressive pedagogies into the curriculum or participating in social movements for racial and class justice, affinity groups have minority students form their own closed support groups defined through identity categories. Affinity groups make solidarity a possibility only for those who share a common experience. Yet, as Keeanga-Yamahta Taylor points out, "solidarity is standing in unity with people even when you have not personally experienced their particular oppression."[11] Distinct from youth groups, affinity groups are being promoted as a social justice remedy justified on the grounds of personal emotional comfort for the oppressed, an affirmation of identity, and a safe space for those who are different to share their experiences. Such therapeutic emotional support comes at the cost of failing to confront the oppressive dimension of the institution while allowing the institution to treat oppression as a problem that starts and ends with the oppressed. By taking an affirmational rather than deconstructive approach to identity, affinity groups tend to make group differences appear to be natural and ahistorical rather than pedagogically constituted, political, and infused with power relations. What is more, the privatized affinity group makes the public problems of oppression and difference topics that cannot be publicly discussed and debated lest the speaker feel discomfort and anxiety. As experience is celebrated as transparently true anchored in the authenticity of identity and the body, these groups largely eschew theory that would facilitate the critical questioning of experience, the identity category, and the relationship between the self and the social. In the logics of personal comfort and psychological trauma, the civic obligation to publicly contest injustice withers, even as the impulse for politics transformed into personal indignation expands. By grounding difference in the body and its affect, and centering the personal and emotion, affinity groups and safe spaces foster modes of social interaction at odds with public culture.

Oddly, at a moment when ubiquitous screens provide readily accessible hyperviolent, exploitative, and sexual imagery, students are traumatized by ordinary speech or university classroom lessons asking students to question themselves and their society.[12] If the safe space is the safe place to speak about contentious or traumatic issues related to identity, then the rest of campus is strung with tripwires that could at any moment unsettle private comforts of selfhood. Again, what is particularly odd about the minefield of identity on campus is that identity (at least gender and sexual identity) is openly recognized as a social construct, performance, and is subject to revision and questioning. What is it that makes such fragility of self out of subjects who have no foundational essence to trouble? Why has emotional comfort and protection from unsettling thought become sacrosanct in public culture? Why has cultural politics become so personalized?

Personalization is in part the result of a culture of atomization fostered by neoliberal ideology, in which the pursuit of self-interest has been successfully made common sense. Yet cultural politics has taken a particular form involving emotion, the body, and a rejection of theory—particularly theory emphasizing that discursive constructs are subject to struggle and that such struggle has educative practice at its core.

These expressions that demand justice do so in forms that presume that culture and politics are private, personal, and bodily affairs. Three factors are contributing to the privatization of cultural politics: the erosion of public space; the remaking of politics through the body; and the related turn back to totalizing identity categories and essentialism in which identity is mistakenly presumed to be self-same, fixed, and grounded in the body rather than discursively constructed, composed of identifications, and subject to rearticulation in part through educative cultural meaning-making work.

Perhaps what has changed since the 1990s is the tendency for liberal guilt and white supremacy to be experienced and expressed in personalized forms that ground the "truth" of race in bodies and feelings. If the demand for privilege checking represents the personalized form of the liberal guilt position, perhaps nothing better illustrates the white supremacist position than the marchers in Charlottesville, Virginia, in 2017 chanting "Jews will not replace us." The perceived threat to white supremacists is existential. The chant highlights the white male fear of physical replacement in the society and workplace and identification of the racial threat as a corporeal one to be destroyed. It is specifically this personalized and corporeal form of race hate that Trump Republicans exploit when targeting Muslims, Mexicans, Blacks, and other minority groups. The proliferation of a sense of physical insecurity and personal anxiety is of course fueled by material conditions that have continued to radically exacerbate inequalities in wealth and income. Economic inequality is accompanied by the gutting of the public sphere and other nonrepressive forms of collective security, such as civil society associations and organizations. Material security is left to the individual who must buy a gun, a gym membership, start a business. The cultural production of symbolic insecurity is overwhelming as well. It ranges from exclusionary social Darwinism, relentless consumerism, (and the feelings of lack it spreads to propagate consumer desire through media culture) to the hypercompetitiveness in education typified by testing fetishism and cutthroat college admissions even as the highest levels of education now guarantee only massive student loan debt but not a career and income.

Material and symbolic precarity and insecurity are fueling subjective states of despair and anxiety. An educational and intellectual crisis is depriving individuals of the intellectual and linguistic means to interpret and comprehend the broader forces and structures producing precarity. The incapacity to name, express, theorize, and comprehend the threats to the self leaves individuals in desperate straits, with little recourse other than numbing the pain or lashing out, often through physical violence. In addition, material and symbolic insecurity and precarity are exacerbated by the market exchange that suggests that all things are moored only by their economic equivalence. As Adorno pointed out, numbers falsely promise material groundings, because the ideology of positivism promotes quantification as having a unique purchase on truth, a promised guarantee of certainty and solidity of things that can be counted.[13]

Similarly, the seeming solidity and certainty of the direct experience of the body offers a false guarantee of truth. The legacy of positivist educational reform has recently begun to locate truth in the body and learning in the flesh through dominant reform policy and technologies, such as biometric pedagogy, grit, smart drugs that reject mediation, dialogue, and thinking in the pedagogical process.[14] The physical grounding of truth is perhaps why the expression of "discomfort" with the discursive positions of others has such power. Or why an experience of disagreement and confrontation with an argument that calls self-certainty into question is increasingly experienced as traumatic and thought to cause harm. The flip side of the same assumption is that a campus speaker ought to be physically assaulted as an existential threat. Rather than contest Charles Murray's eugenic arguments with better arguments, protesters beat him up as if the argument and the body are the same thing.[15] As rational public discourse becomes a perilous proposition and safe harbor can only be sought in the private shelter of the safe space and the body, the public is opened to bigots who promise to use their strong bodies to protect weak ones and to annihilate those bodies deemed a threat.

In this chapter, I criticize privatized and personalized forms of culture and educational politics that fuel the racial defensiveness, pride, and essentialism that also lend themselves to the white supremacy and reactionary politics that they seek to counter. These privatized forms of culture do so by essentializing racial identity, collapsing ideology and identity, and refusing to admit that identity and consciousness are pedagogically constituted and open to remaking. By collapsing white identity with white supremacist ideology, shame, and guilt, they leave no possibility for whiteness to be rearticulated in antiracist and radically democratic forms. In such an articulation, the particular struggle for antiracism is linked to other imbricated struggles for justice and equality.

In contrast to the privatized cultural politics discussed in this chapter, the Black Lives Matter protests of the summer of 2020 demonstrated a *public* demand for racial justice. Videos of police killings of unarmed Black people circulated and enabled public witness to the horror of state violence that disproportionately targets Black citizens. People took to the street all across the United States and around the world. Whites and other non-Black people marched and put up public signs declaring their solidarity with the movement. The power of the images of racial violence had to do in part with their ability to bring to public view what power had previously been able to conceal. This effort built on a legacy of imagery revealing concealed racial violence in, for example, photographic documentation of lynchings, film footage shown on television of the attacks on freedom riders in the 1960s, and the display of Emmett Till's mutilated body. The videos of the murders of George Floyd and many others concretized the abstraction of racialized state violence and allowed for the identification of the viewer with the victims of police murder. However, these videos and the bodies in them did not become meaningful on their own. Black Lives Matter and other social justice movements needed to interpolate the imagery into a broader narrative of social criticism and social imagination and possibility. These movements acted publicly, politically, and pedagogically to educate others to a new recognition of racialized violence, the structural and systemic dimension of that violence, and to open up questions about the purposes and roles of both repressive and caregiving public institutions in a democratic society.

CONCLUSION

This book has shown how increasing precarity, inequality, and crises of agency have resulted in Americans desperately grasping for certainty and concreteness in the forms of numbers and bodies. I have shown how decades of neoliberal educational restructuring and the continued embrace of positivism has created the educational conditions for the willingness to treat fact as a matter of the assertion of the strong, and to delink fact from the theories and arguments that make it meaningful. I have also shown how new forms of digital educational privatization are continuing and deepening the long-standing uses of positivism in public schooling. These trends are encouraging students to understand knowledge and the process of learning in ways that are divorced from understanding and acting on the self and society.

The phenomena illustrated in this book need to be comprehended as part of broader social, economic, political, cultural, technological, and educational tendencies that are subject to struggle and contestation. As the philosopher Antonio Gramsci suggested, the dominant hegemonic bloc must not only educate others to its particular ideological common sense as the universal in order to win social dominance. To hold the social order, the dominant bloc must also ongoingly pedagogically produce its particular hegemonic common sense as the universal. It is crucial to comprehend the uses of positivism to

claim disinterested objectivity in education, culture, and technology in these political terms of contested hegemonic control by classes and cultural groups. I have argued throughout
this book that what is at stake in contests over cultural meanings and the ownership and control over cultural institutions
is the struggle for a radically democratic society.

Also, what is at stake in rejecting the new articulations of
positivism promoted by digital privatization of education is
the capacity to see education as a means of making a society
of thinking people who are capable of comprehending claims
to truth in relation to the social authority of the claimant,
their interests, social location, and their ideological positions,
values, and assumptions. It is crucial to expand the capacity
of thinking people to comprehend not just the society and
the self but also knowledge and learning as a means of collective self-governance. Such comprehension demands the
use of theory, not just more facts or better facts. The educational task ahead must centrally include providing people
with the intellectual tools and traditions to interpret experience. As Theodor Adorno points out when explaining the
allure of positivism, "our world is so dominated by abstract
regularities, and the relationships between people have themselves become so abstract, that the concrete has become a
kind of utopia."[1] The abstract regularities to which Adorno
refers include the ways that capitalism transforms everything
into an economic exchange relation with a quantified value.
This abstraction includes not only the transformation of relations between people into money equivalences but also data,
digital, and televisual abstraction. The growing fetishization
of fact and data and the concreteness of bodies and numbers obscure underlying values, assumptions, ideologies, and
theories that organize knowledge and make it meaningful. It
mistakenly treats immediate experience as a final arbiter of
truth and positions a dynamic social reality as static. There
is no place in this view for the negation of existing reality

to imagine a different, better future. Nor is there a place for learning to involve comprehending the values, assumptions, ideologies, and interests that undergird claims to truth and the ways that interpretations fit into broader constellations of power, social tendencies, and structures. Educational projects, such as critical pedagogy, in conjunction with social movements and other meaning-making practices can contribute to the development of critical consciousness and the democratic imagination, so that acts of interpretation can contribute to ethical and political comprehension of social reality and the possibility for collective social action.

The response to these precarious economic, political, and cultural conditions and forces has to be the development of more public forms of democracy in more places. That means not just safeguarding liberal electoral democracy but also expanding democratic social relations in all institutions of the political system, culture, and economy. It also means developing the democratic potential in producing and consuming critical and publicly owned and accessed iterations of technology by expanding new forms of critical media literacies and political economic analysis in the realms of artificial intelligence and big data. The ideas that I have sought to hammer home harder than any other in this book is that education, in its various positivist and neoliberal forms, contributes to the contemporary crisis of truth and politics, and it undermines the capacity of people to enact a democratic society. Education, curriculum, and pedagogy are always inevitably political, because they are engaged in making meanings, affirming or contesting particular discourses, and producing points of identification. A society theoretically committed to democracy must realize the potential in forms of schooling and educational projects that can provide the intellectual tools and traditions to make learning the basis for social and self-interpretation, understanding, and agency.

Another crucial idea that I have emphasized in the book is that technology always contains embedded values, assumptions, and ideologies that are often misrepresented as outside of cultural politics—beyond human examination, understanding, and control. Part of what my book calls for in the future are forms of critical education that can teach people how to analyze the values, assumptions, and ideologies embedded in technologies as well as the knowledge and curriculum that such technologies host. Such a critical approach to new technology must involve projects that explore the critical capacities of technologies to counter the alienation of social relationships, better understand the relations between objects and human subjects, and expose the power relations among groups and classes that are often concealed in the guise of objectivity.

NOTES

PREFACE

1. On the precarity being produced by global capitalism, see, for example, William I. Robinson, *Into the Tempest: Essays on the New Global Capitalism* (Chicago: Haymarket Books, 2018); and William I. Robinson, *The Global Police State* (London: Pluto Press, 2020). On the existential threats of global warming, nuclear annihilation, and capitalism, see also Noam Chomsky and Marv Waterstone, *Consequences of Capitalism: Manufacturing Discontent and Resistance* (Chicago: Haymarket Press, 2021).

2. Robert McChesney, *Digital Disconnect: How Capitalism Is Turning the Internet against Democracy* (New York: The New Press, 2013). On the authoritarian assault on journalism, see Jason Stanley, *How Fascism Works: The Politics of Us and Them* (New York: Random House, 2018); Timothy Snyder, *On Tyranny: Twenty Lessons from the Twentieth Century* (New York: Crown, 2017).

3. Martin Gilens and Benjamin I. Page, "Testing Theories of American Politics: Elites, Interest Groups, and Average Citizens," *Perspectives on Politics* 12, no. 3 (2014): 564–581. "Multivariate analysis indicates that economic elites and organized groups representing business interests have substantial independent impacts on U.S. government policy, while average citizens and mass-based interest groups have little or no independent influence."

4. Henry A. Giroux, *The Terror of Neoliberalism: Authoritarianism and the Eclipse of Democracy* (Boulder: Paradigm Publishers, 2004). Stanley, *How*

Fascism Works; Snyder, *On Tyranny*. The Republican party in the United States has reoriented its political platform on multiple antidemocracy positions and laws—most notably, voter suppression, efforts to criminalize protest and dissent, and promotion of censorship and anti-free speech laws.

5. Nancy Fraser, *The Old Is Dying and the New Cannot Be Born* (London: Verso, 2019).

6. William I. Robinson, "Global Capitalism Post-Pandemic," *Race & Class* 62, no. 2 (2020): 3–13.

7. Robinson, "Global Capitalism Post-Pandemic."

8. Henry A. Giroux, *Education and the Crisis of Public Values* (New York: Peter Lang, 2012); Kenneth J. Saltman, *The Failure of Corporate School Reform* (New York: Routledge, 2012); David Hursh, *The End of Public Schools: The Corporate Reform Agenda to Privatize Education* (New York: Routledge, 2015); Alexander Means, *Schooling in the Age of Austerity* (New York: Palgrave Macmillan, 2014).

9. I take up the relationship between corporatization of education and repression in several books, including Kenneth J. Saltman, *Capitalizing on Disaster: Taking and Breaking Public Schools* (New York: Routledge, 2007), and Kenneth J. Saltman, *Scripted Bodies: Corporate Power, Smart Technologies, and the Undoing of Public Education* (New York: Routledge, 2016). See also Giroux, *Education and the Crisis of Public Values*; Hursh, *The End of Public Schools*.

10. Zygmunt Bauman, *Strangers at Our Door* (Malden, MA: Polity, 2016).

11. In this book I use the expression "Strongmen" to mark the revived masculinism utilized by these leaders as well as to point out that nearly all if not all are men. Trump, Putin, Duterte, Bolsonaro and so on make masculinity integral to the promise of strength and security and the threat of violence. As well, the term highlights the extent to which this form of authoritarian leadership involves often hyperbolic performance of aggressive masculinity like that of the strongman at the circus.

12. As Cris Shore describes it, audit culture "refers to contexts in which the techniques and values of accountancy have become a central organizing principle in the governance and management

of human conduct—and the new kinds of relationships, habits and practices that this is creating" (Cris Shore, "Audit Culture and Illiberal Governance," *Anthropological Theory* 8, no. 3 (2008): 278–298, 279). In neoliberal educational contexts, such audit culture saturates the norms of administration and teaching with imperatives for quantified progress applied to pedagogy, curriculum, and as I detail here, student behavior. Mark Fisher's discussion in *Capitalist Realism: Is There No Alternative?* (London: Zero Books, 2009) of audit culture as a mandatory performance of quantified efficacy further describes the disconnection between meaningful progress grounded in public and human values and principles and the mushrooming requirements that teachers, administrators, and students make a show of quantified progress. The point not to be missed is that the display of the quantification of progress stands in for the thoughtful enactment of socially meaningful forms of teaching, learning, and the management of schools. Fisher calls this phony performance of efficacy "market Stalinism." I have discussed this in the context of the new market bureaucracy in education. Under the guise of reducing bureaucracy through the natural efficiencies of markets, an entirely new market bureaucracy has been rolled out with global, national, regional, and local nonprofit and for-profit institutions. This market bureaucracy is dedicated to transforming public education into private markets, in part through the discourse of human capital and the translation of all aspects of education into metrics to naturalize the restricted economic purposes of public schooling. See Saltman, *The Failure of Corporate School Reform.*

13. Kim Parker, "The Growing Partisan Divide in Views of Higher Education," Pew Research Center (January 30, 2019). https://www .pewresearch.org/social-trends/2019/08/19/the-growing-partisan -divide-in-views-of-higher-education-2/.

14. Cary Funk, Brian Kennedy, and Courtney Johnson, "Trust in Medical Scientists Has Grown in U.S., but Mainly among Democrats," Pew Research Center (May 21, 2020). https://www.pewresearch.org /science/2020/05/21/trust-in-medical-scientists-has-grown-in-u-s-but -mainly-among-democrats/.

15. Catherine Kim, "Poll: 70 Percent of Republicans Don't Think Election Was Free and Fair," *Politico*, November 9, 2020; Ellen Cranley,

"These Are the 130 Current Members of Congress Who Have Doubted or Denied Climate Change," *Business Insider,* April 29, 2019.

16. I review the lack of evidence for and evidence against multiple market-based school reforms (including charters, vouchers, and urban portfolio districts) in Saltman, *The Failure of Corporate School Reform.* See also Martin Carnoy, "School Vouchers Are Not a Proven Strategy for Improving Student Achievement," Economic Policy Institute, February 28, 2017. http://www.epi.org/publication/school-vouchers -are-not-a-proven-strategy-for-improving-student-achievement/. For a recent review of the lack of evidence supporting online remote learning (which vastly expanded during the COVID-19 global pandemic), see A. Molnar (ed.), G. Miron, M. K. Barbour, L. Huerta, S. R. Shafer, J. K. Rice, A. Glover et al. "Virtual Schools in the U.S. 2021" (Boulder: National Education Policy Center, 2021). http://nepc.colorado.edu /publication/virtual-schools-annual-2021.

17. The obvious source of this idea is Max Horkheimer and Theodor Adorno, *Dialectic of Enlightenment* (Stanford, CA: Stanford University Press, 2002). In various chapters, I draw specifically on Adorno's insights about the allure of positivism as the false promise of concreteness. Theodor Adorno, *Introduction to Sociology* (Stanford, CA: Stanford University Press, 2000), 49, states: "If you consider the role played . . . by the concept of the concrete in value-free, positivist sociology, you can get some sense of the curious affective charge which has attached itself to this term. The most likely reason . . . is that our world is so dominated by abstract regularities, and the relationships between people have themselves become so abstract, that the concrete has become a kind of utopia."

18. Megen Feren, "Remote Learning and School Reopenings: What Worked and What Didn't," Center for American Progress, July 6, 2021. https://www.americanprogress.org/issues/education-k-12/reports/2021 /07/06/501221/remote-learning-school-reopenings-worked-didnt/.

   Natasha Singer, "Learning Apps Have Boomed in the Pandemic. Now Here Comes the Real Test," *New York Times,* March 17, 2021.

19. Ben Williamson, Rebecca Eynon, and John Potter, "Pandemic Politics, Pedagogies and Practices: Digital Technologies and Distance

Education during the Coronavirus Emergency," *Learning Media and Technology* 45, no. 2 (May 2020): 107–114.

20. Valerie Strauss, "Cuomo Questions Why School Buildings Still Exist—And Says New York Will Work with Bill Gates to 'Reimagine Education,'" *Washington Post,* May 6, 2020.

21. John P. Bailey, Frederick M. Hess, Chris Cerf, Carrie Conaway, Sharif El-Mekki, Dale Erquiaga, Kaya Henderson et al., "A Blueprint for Back to School," American Enterprise Institute, 2020; Jason Bedrick and Matthew Ladner, "Let's Get Small: Microschools, Pandemic Pods, and the Future of Education in America," The Heritage Foundation, October 6, 2020; Michael B. Horn, "The Rapid Rise of Pandemic Pods," *Education Next* 21, no. 1 (Winter 2021).

22. Martin Carnoy, "School Vouchers Are Not a Proven Strategy for Improving Student Achievement," Economic Policy Institute, February 28, 2017. https://www.epi.org/publication/school-vouchers -are-not-a-proven-strategy-for-improving-student-achievement/; K. G. Welner, *Neovouchers: The Emergence of Tuition Tax Credits for Private Schooling* (Lanham, MD: Rowman & Littlefield, 2008).

23. Alicia Inez Guzman, "You've Reached 17,494 Students Please Leave a Message," *Searchlight New Mexico,* August 18, 2021.

24. Jathan Sadowski, "When Data Is Capital: Datafication, Accumulation, and Extraction," *Big Data and Society* (January–June 2019): 1–12.

25. Molnar et al., "Virtual Schools in the U.S. 2021."

26. Positivism as a philosophy originates with August Compte, the founder of sociology. The Frankfurt School of Critical Theory and most significantly, Theodor Adorno, criticized positivism in multiple places, including Adorno, *Introduction to Sociology*; Theodor Adorno, *Lectures on Negative Dialectics,* ed. Rolf Tiedemann, trans. Rodney Livingstone (Malden, MA: Polity, 2008); and Horkheimer and Adorno, *Dialectic of Enlightenment.* See also Max Horkheimer's *Critical Theory (New York: Continuum, 2002).* Since the Frankfurt School, some key social philosophers have built on these insights, including Richard J. Bernstein, Zygmunt Bauman, and Stanley Aronowitz. In education, Henry Giroux has built on these criticisms of positivism to analyze schooling.

27. Adorno, *Introduction to Sociology,* 48–49.

28. Samuel Bowles and Herbert Gintis, *Schooling in Capitalist America* (Chicago: Haymarket, 2011) (originally published in 1976).

29. Henry Giroux's scholarship from the 1970s and 1980s provided crucial analysis of the culture of positivism in public education during the industrial era. See, for example, Henry A. Giroux, *Theory and Resistance in Education* (Westport, CT: Bergin & Garvey 1983); and Henry A. Giroux, "Schooling and the Culture of Positivism," *Educational Theory* 29, no. 4 (1979), 263–284.

30. Paulo Freire, *Pedagogy of the Oppressed* (New York: Continuum, 1972).

31. Robinson, *The Global Police State.*

32. My prior two books, Saltman, *Scripted Bodies,* and Kenneth J. Saltman, *The Swindle of Innovative Educational Finance* (Minneapolis: University of Minnesota Press, 2018), are both studies of this phenomenon of the intersections of "innovative finance" and technologies of corporeal control in education.

33. I detail these framings of impact investors with the case of Social Impact Bonds in Saltman, *The Swindle of Innovative Educational Finance.* To watch a chilling illustration of contemporary uses of positivist ideology and the dream of impact investors to transform all of the human and natural world into quantification for capitalist investment, see "IXO: The Blockchain for Impact" video, https://vimeo.com /264055837. The promise made in the video is of transforming everything into numbers to save the world with more capitalism from the very effects of capitalism: global warming, poverty, and so forth. See Adorno's important discussion of how positivism prohibits thinking while appealing to advancement in his *Introduction to Sociology,* 45.

CHAPTER 1

1. Three major new studies of vouchers were released at the start of 2017 that joined with other studies and international studies from Chile and India to paint an utterly damning picture of the empirical case for vouchers. See Martin Carnoy, "School Vouchers Are Not a Proven Strategy for Improving Student Achievement," Economic Policy Institute,

February 28, 2017. http://www.epi.org/publication/school-vouchers -are-not-a-proven-strategy-for-improving-student-achievement/.

2. Zygmunt Bauman, *Strangers at Our Door* (New York: Polity, 2016).

3. Frederick Taylor, *The Principles of Scientific Management* (New York: Harper and Brothers, 1911); John Franklin Bobbitt was the leading figure of the educational efficiency movement. On the importation of scientific management into education, see Herbert Kliebard, *The Struggle for the American Curriculum, 1893–1958,* third edition (New York: Routledge, 2004).

4. See, for example, Stephen Jay Gould, *The Mismeasure of Man* (New York: Norton, 1996) and a contemporary dissection of the application of these ideas in Mark Garrison, *A Measure of Failure* (Albany, NY: SUNY Press, 2009).

5. This point on the possibility of schooling and informal educative encounters to be sites of resistance and counterhegemonic struggle has been made by Antonio Gramsci, Paulo Freire, Samuel Bowles, Herbert Gintis, Stanley Aronowitz, Henry Giroux, and bell hooks, among others. See Henry A. Giroux, *Theory and Resistance in Education* (Westport, CT: Bergin & Garvey, 1983).

6. See Paulo Freire, *Pedagogy of the Oppressed* (New York: Continuum, 1972), and Giroux, *Theory and Resistance in Education.*

7. See David Berliner and Bruce Biddle, *The Manufactured Crisis* (New York: Basic Books, 1996) and more recently, Gene Glass and David Berliner, *50 Myths and Lies That Threaten America's Public Schools: The Real Crisis in Education* (New York: Teachers College Press, 2014).

8. See the discussion of the CZI, philanthrocapitalism, and personalized learning in Kenneth Saltman, *The Swindle of Innovative Educational Finance* (Minneapolis: University of Minnesota Press, 2018).

9. Caitlin Emma, Benjamin Wermund, and Kimberly Helfing et al., "DeVos' Michigan Schools Experiment Gets Poor Grades," *Politico.* http://www.politico.com/story/2016/12/betsy-devos-michigan-school -experiment-232399. For a review of the educational policy scholarship in terms of a broader advocacy of critical education, see Kenneth Saltman, *The Failure of Corporate School Reform* (New York: Routledge, 2012).

10. Carnoy, "School Vouchers Are Not a Proven Strategy for Improving Student Achievement."

11. John P. Bailey, Frederick M. Hess, Chris Cerf, Carrie Conaway, Sharif El-Mekki, Dale Erquiaga, Kaya Henderson et al., "A Blueprint for Back to School," American Enterprise Institute, 2020; Jason Bedrick and Matthew Ladner, "Let's Get Small: Microschools, Pandemic Pods, and the Future of Education in America," The Heritage Foundation, October 6, 2020; Michael B. Horn, "The Rapid Rise of Pandemic Pods," *Education Next* 21, no. 1 (Winter 2021). Carnoy, "School Vouchers Are Not a Proven Strategy for Improving Student Achievement." K. G. Welner, *Neovouchers: The Emergence of Tuition Tax Credits for Private Schooling* (Lanham, MD: Rowman & Littlefield, 2008).

12. Andy Smarick, "The Turnaround Fallacy: Stop Trying to Fix Failing Schools. Close Them and Start Fresh" *Education Next* 10, no. 1 (Winter 2010). http://educationnext.org/the-turnaround-fallacy/.

13. Paul T. Hill, Christine Campbell, David Menefee-Libey, Brianna Dusseault, Michael DeArmond, Betheny Gross, et al., "Portfolio School Districts for Big Cities: An Interim Report," Center on Reinventing Public Education, October 2009. Saltman, *The Failure of Corporate School Reform.*

14. David Leonhardt, "A Plea for a Fact-Based Debate about Charter Schools," *New York Times,* July 22, 2018. Sean F. Reardon and Rebecca Hinze-Pifer, "Test Score Growth among Chicago Public School Students 2009–2014," Stanford Center for Education Policy Analysis, November 2017.

15. See the National Assessment of Educational Progress report card. https://www.nationsreportcard.gov/.

16. Pierre Bourdieu, "The Forms of Capital," in *Handbook of Theory and Research for the Sociology of Education,* ed. J. Richardson (New York: Greenwood, 1986): 241–258.

17. Mark Fisher, *Capitalist Realism* (London: Zero Books, 2009).

18. Fact Checker, *Washington Post,* January 24, 2021. https://www.washingtonpost.com/politics/2021/01/24/trumps-false-or-misleading-claims-total-30573-over-four-years/.

19. Caitlin Emma, Benjamin Wermund, and Kimberly Helfing, "DeVos' Michigan Schools Experiment Gets Poor Grades," *Politico*. http://www.politico.com/story/2016/12/betsy-devos-michigan-school-experiment-232399.

20. Ulrich Boser, "Betsy DeVos Has Invested Millions in This Brain Training Center. So I Checked It Out," *Washington Post*, May 26, 2017. https://www.washingtonpost.com/posteverything/wp/2017/05/26/betsy-devos-neurocore/?utm_term=.366a865e3c3d.

21. Caitlin Moniz, "Betsy DeVos Did Not Issue a Recusal Statement for Matters Involving Neurocore," CREW, June 7, 2019. https://www.citizensforethics.org/reports-investigations/crew-investigations/devos-neurocore-recusal-conflict/.

22. See Robert McChesney, *Digital Disconnect: How Capitalism Is Turning the Internet against Democracy* (New York: The New Press, 2013).

23. Susan McWilliams, "This Political Theorist Predicted the Rise of Trumpism: His Name Was Hunter S. Thompson," *The Nation*, December 15, 2016.

24. Theodor W. Adorno, *History and Freedom: Lectures 1964–1965* (Malden, MA: Polity 2008), 30.

25. Adorno, *History and Freedom*, 40.

26. Theodor W. Adorno, *Introduction to Sociology* (Stanford, CA: Stanford University Press, 2000), 32.

27. Adorno, *Introduction to Sociology*, 39.

28. Adorno, *Introduction to Sociology*, 45. Marx contends in the "Economic and Philosophic Manuscripts of 1844" Karl Marx & Frederick Engels, "Economic and Philosophic Manuscripts of 1844" in Robert C. Tucker (ed.) The Marx-Engels Reader, Second Edition (New York: W.W. Norton & Co., 1978) that when the material conditions force the worker to face their brutal life conditions, ideology falls away, and the real conditions will be grasped. Of course, Adorno and the other Frankfurt School theorists reject the false consciousness model and comprehend that ideology does not fall away. Instead, experience is always mediated through ideologies—such as positivism. Particular identity positions (e.g., workers, students, inmates) cannot be

presumed to be inherently liberatory. Experience demands theorization. If we are saturated in ideology, the educational and political question is: What kinds of ideologies are preferable to others?

29. Adorno distinguished science from scientism or a fetishization of science and scientific method that he explained as an expression of positivist ideology. He states, "I understand fetishism in science to mean that science, with its specific form of argumentation and immanent methods, becomes an end in itself, without any relation to its subject matter" (Adorno, *Introduction to Sociology*, 127–128). Adorno explains that positivism denies concepts and hence thought (Adorno, *Introduction to Sociology*, 79) and fosters practicism in service to the preservation of existing oppressive social systems Adorno, *Introduction to Sociology*, 26).

30. Pierre Bourdieu and Jean Passeron, *Reproduction in Education Society and Culture* (Thousand Oaks, CA: Sage, 1990). Henry Giroux's *Theory and Resistance in Education* provides a valuable engagement with the limitations of Bourdieu's emphasis on structural determinations for theorizing critical consciousness, resistance, agency, and critical educational practice.

31. Erich Fromm, *Escape from Freedom* (London: Routledge, Keegan & Paul, 1941).

CHAPTER 2

1. Virginia Eubanks, *Automating Inequality* (New York: St. Martin's Press, 2017); Cathy O'Neil, *Weapons of Math Destruction* (New York: Broadway Books, 2016).

2. Shoshana Zuboff, *The Age of Surveillance Capitalism* (New York: Public Affairs, 2019).

3. Neil Selwyn, *Should Robots Replace Teachers? AI and the Future of Education* (Medford, MA: Polity Press, 2019), 22.

4. White House Report, "Preparing for the Future of Artificial Intelligence." Executive Office of the President, National Science and Technology Council Committee on Technology, 1–48. https://obamawhitehouse .archives.gov/sites/default/files/whitehouse_files/microsites/ostp/NSTC /preparing_for_the_future_of_ai.pdf, 7.

5. White House Report, "Preparing for the Future of Artificial Intelligence," 7.

6. Ben Williamson, J. Pykett, and S. Nemorin, "Biosocial Spaces and Neurocomputational Governance: Brain-Based and Brain-Targeted Technologies in Education," *Discourse: Studies in the Cultural Politics of Education* 39, no. 2 (2017): 258–275, 266.

7. Kenneth J. Saltman, *Scripted Bodies: Corporate Power, Smart Technologies, and the Undoing of Public Education* (New York: Routledge, 2016), 74–95.

8. Alexander J. Means, *Learning to Save the Future* (New York: Routledge, 2019), 6.

9. Faith Boninger, Alex Molnar, and C. Saldana, "Personalized Learning and the Digital Privatization of Curriculum and Teaching," National Education Policy Center (April 2019), 10. http://nepc.colorado.edu/publication/personalized-learning; J. F. Pane, "Strategies for Implementing Personalized Learning while Evidence and Resources Are Underdeveloped" (Santa Monica, CA: Rand Corporation 2018), 4.

10. Slavoj Zizek, *Like a Thief in Broad Daylight* (London: Allen Lane, 2018), 14.

11. Boninger, Molnar, and Saldana, "Personalized Learning and the Digital Privatization of Curriculum"; Jathan Sadowski, "When Data Is Capital: Datafication, Accumulation, and Extraction," *Big Data and Society* (January–June 2019): 1–12; Jamie Manolev, Anna Sullivan, and Roger Slee, "The Datafication of Discipline: Class Dojo, Surveillance and a Performative Classroom Culture," *Learning, Media and Technology* 44, no. 1 (2018): 36–51.

12. Boninger, Molnar, and Saldana, "Personalized Learning and the Digital Privatization of Curriculum," 21.

13. Boninger, Molnar, and Saldana, "Personalized Learning and the Digital Privatization of Curriculum," 10.

14. Kenneth J. Saltman, *The Swindle of Innovative Educational Finance* (Minneapolis: University of Minnesota Press, 2018), 53–74.

15. See a sample of the Summit Learning curriculum at: https://www.summitlearning.org/guest/courses.

16. Nellie Bowles and Natasha Singer, "Silicon Valley Came to Kansas, It Didn't Go Well," *New York Times,* April 21, 2019.

17. Summit, on its website, represents the curriculum as integral to the platform. However, while the skills and rubric appear to be universals, some teachers have largely replaced the curriculum. There is a question as to the extent to which teachers can use the technology "off label." That is, to what extent can the technology platform be open to use for critical curriculum projects? Yet the form that teaching takes, with the use of Summit oriented to constant testing, quantification of what passes for learning, measurement, and control accords with the way that Summit targets working class and predominantly African American and Latinx student populations and communities. Such pedagogies of control appear not to be winning over professional class school districts. This speaks to the extent to which Summit and other repressive pedagogies are implicated in social and cultural reproduction of the racialized class hierarchy—for the sake of making disciplined and docile future workers.

18. Jocalyn Clark and Linsey McGoey, "The Black Box Warning on Philanthrocapitalism," *The Lancet* 388 (2016): 2457–2459; Daniel Dykes and Michael S. Schwartz, "The Chan Zuckerberg Initiative," *Trusts and Estates* (May 2016); Martin Levine, "Chan Zuckerberg LLC: No Tax Breaks + No Accountability = What Exactly?" *Non-Profit Quarterly,* December 7, 2015; Natasha Singer and Mike Isaac, "Mark Zuckerberg's Philanthropy Uses L.L.C. for More Control," *New York Times,* December 2, 2015; Sindhu Kashyap, "Why BYJU's Chose to Bet on Edurite and Tutorvista," *Your Story,* May 15, 2017, https://yourstory.com/2017/05/byjus -edurite-tutorvista/; Sayan Chakraborty, "BYJU's Updates App, Aims to Make Profits This Year," *LiveMint,* May 24, 2017, https://www.livemint .com/Companies/W0pmP4tPipqmo8ozq9lMDJ/Byjus-updates-app -aims-to-make-profits-this-year.html; Faith Boninger, Alex Molnar, and Kevin Murray, "Asleep at the Switch: Schoolhouse Commercialism, Student Privacy, and the Failure of Policymaking," *National Education Policy Center,* August 2017, http://nepc.colorado.edu/publication/schoolhouse -commercialism-2017; Emma Brown and Todd C. Frankel, "Facebook Backed School Software Shows Promise—and Raises Privacy Concerns," *Washington Post,* October 11, 2016, https://www.washingtonpost.com /local/education/facebook-backed-school-software-shows-promise -and-raises-privacy-concerns/2016/10/11/2580f9fe-80c6-11e6-b002

-307601806392_story.html; Summit's user agreement with schools is available at https://drive.google.com/file/d/0B4_mvdmEmtsTYXF4M 3RUb1hLalE/view. Natasha Singer, "The Silicon Valley Billionaires Remaking America's Schools," *New York Times*, June 6, 2017.

19. Kenneth J. Saltman, *The Gift of Education: Public Education and Venture Philanthropy* (New York: Palgrave Macmillan, 2010).

20. Saltman, *Scripted Bodies*, 55–73.

21. I detail Social Impact Bonds/Pay for Success in Saltman, *Swindle of Innovative Educational Finance*, 25–42.

22. Melissa Sanchez, "Investors Earn Max Initial Payment from Chicago's 'Social Impact Bond,'" *Chicago Reporter*, May 16, 2016, https://www.chicagoreporter.com/investors-earn-max-initial-payment-from -chicagos-social-impact-bond/.

23. Saltman, *Swindle of Innovative Educational Finance,* 33.

24. Wrench in the Gears (blog), "Third Grade Reading Guarantees: Impact Investors Build System to Terrorize Eight Year Olds," February 27, 2019. https://wrenchinthegears.com/2019/02/27/3rd-grade-reading -guarantees-impact-investors-build-system-to-terrorize-eight-year-olds/.

25. Ben Williamson and Nelli Piattoeva, "Objectivity as Standardization in Data-Scientific Education Policy, Technology and Governance," *Learning, Media and Technology* 44, no. 1 (2019): 74.

26. Samuel Bowles and Herbert Gintis, *Schooling in Capitalist America* (Chicago: Haymarket Press, 2011): 79. (Originally published in 1976.)

27. Singer, "The Silicon Valley Billionaires Remaking America's Schools," A1.

28. H. Kronk, "Johns Hopkins Researchers Found 'Significant Problems' with Summit Learning Use in Providence Schools," *E-Learning Inside,* July 1, 2019. https://news.elearninginside.com/johns-hopkins -researchers-found-significant-problems-with-summit-learning-use-in -providence-schools/.

29. On the repressive tendencies of neoliberal capitalism and capitalism more generally, particularly with regard to political economy and social and cultural reproduction, see David Harvey, *A Brief History*

of Neoliberalism (Oxford: Oxford University Press, 2007); William I. Robinson, *The Global Police State* (London: Pluto Press, 2020); Noam Chomsky and Marv Waterstone, *Consequences of Capitalism: Manufacturing Discontent and Resistance* (Chicago: Haymarket Books, 2021). I have discussed this tendency in education in various books, including Saltman, *Scripted Bodies*, 1–17.

30. Dallas Smyth, "On the Audience Commodity and Its Work," in *Dependency Road: Communications, Capitalism, Consciousness, and Canada* (Norwood, NJ: Ablex, 1981), 22–51.

31. Sadowski, "When Data Is Capital," 2.

32. Ruha Benjamin, *Race after Technology: Abolitionist Tools for the New Jim Code* (London: Polity, 2020), 5.

33. Benjamin, *Race after Technology*, 7.

34. Stuart Hall, *Representation: Cultural Representations and Signifying Practices* (Thousand Oaks, CA: Sage, 1997), 15–63.

35. Henry A. Giroux, *On Critical Pedagogy* (New York: Continuum, 2011): 19–47; Kenneth J. Saltman, "Antitheory, Positivism, and Critical Pedagogy," in *What's Wrong with Anti-Theory*, ed. J. R. Di Leo (New York: Bloomsbury, 2020), 73–91.

36. Theodor Adorno. *Introduction to Sociology*, ed. Christoph Gödde, trans. Edmund Jephcott (Stanford, CA: Stanford University Press, 2000), 75.

37. Henry A. Giroux, *Theory and Resistance in Education* (Westport, CT: Bergin & Garvey, 1983), 58–59.

CHAPTER 3

1. The Centervention Zoo U website is available at https://www .centervention.com/social-skills-game/.

2. Jamie Manolev, Anna Sullivan, and Roger Slee, "The Datafication of Discipline: Class Dojo, Surveillance and a Performative Classroom Culture," *Learning, Media and Technology* 44, no. 1 (2018): 1–16.

3. Kenneth J. Saltman, *Scripted Bodies: Corporate Power, Smart Technologies, and the Undoing of Public Education* (New York: Routledge, 2016), 55–73.

4. Jill Barshay, "Impact Funds Pour Money into Ed Tech Businesses," *Hechinger Report*, October 21, 2019.

5. Ben Williamson and Nelli Piattoeva, "Objectivity as Standardization in Data-Scientific Education Policy, Technology, and Governance," *Learning, Media and Technology* 44, no. 1 (2019): 64–76; Kenneth J. Saltman and Alexander J. Means (eds.), *The Wiley Handbook of Global Educational Reform* (Medford, MA: Wiley Blackwell, 2019).

6. Valerie Strauss detailed the millions of dollars educational publishers invested in lobbying for testing and the billions they reaped as a result. See Valerie Strauss, "Big Education Firms Spend Millions Lobbying for Pro-Testing Policies," *Washington Post*, March 30, 2015.

7. Saltman, *Scripted Bodies*.

8. World Economic Forum, "Schools of the Future: Defining New Models of Education for the Fourth Industrial Revolution," www.weforum .org (January 2020): 1–33; Williamson and Piattoeva, "Objectivity as Standardization in Data-Scientific Education Policy."

9. Barshay, "Impact Funds Pour Money into Ed Tech Businesses," 6.

10. Barshay, "Impact Funds Pour Money into Ed Tech Businesses."

11. William I. Robinson, *Into the Tempest* (Chicago: Haymarket, 2018): 11–29.

12. Robinson, *Into the Tempest*, 11–12.

13. In the United States alone, education has been valued as a $1.5 trillion per year sector that is ripe for privatization. See Jake Bryant and Jimmy Sarakatsannis, "Why US Education Is Ready for Investment" (New York: McKinsey & Company), July 2015.

14. I have written extensively on neoliberal educational restructuring. See, for example, Kenneth J. Saltman, *The Failure of Corporate School Reform* (New York: Routledge, 2012).

15. Educational finance scholar Bruce Baker contends that the charter municipal bond bubble stands to burst, resulting in a potential trillion-dollar debt crisis. See his "Picture Post Week: Subprime Chartering (blog), School Finance 101, December 10, 2015. https:// schoolfinance101.wordpress.com/2015/12/10/picture-post-week -subprime-chartering/.

16. See Nick Couldry and Ulises A. Meijas, *The Costs of Connection: How Data Is Colonizing Human Life and Appropriating It for Capitalism* (Stanford, CA: Stanford University Press, 2019).

17. OECD, "Social and Emotional Skills: Well-Being, Connectedness, and Success" (Paris: OECD); World Economic Forum, "Schools of the Future."

18. Valerie Strauss, "Cuomo Questions Why School Buildings Still Exist—and Says New York Will Work with Bill Gates to 'Reimagine Education,'" *Washington Post,* May 6, 2020. For an excellent early scholarly response to the misuse of the pandemic to advance the commercial agenda in education, see Ben Williamson, Rebecca Enyon, and John Potter, "Pandemic Politics, Pedagogies and Practices: Digital Technologies and Distance Education during the Coronavirus Emergency," *Learning Media and Technology,* May 21, 2020.

19. Secretary of Education Betsy DeVos directed public education coronavirus relief money to private and religious schools; see Erica L. Green, "DeVos Funnels Coronavirus Relief Funds to Favored Private and Religious Schools," *New York Times,* May 15, 2020.

20. The unbundling agenda of right wing think tanks is on display, for example, in Frederick Hess, Bruno Manno, and Olivia Meeks at the American Enterprise Institute in "From School Choice to Educational Choice." https://www.aei.org/research-products/report/from-school-choice-to -educational-choice/.

21. Jathan Sadowski, "When Data Is Capital: Datafication, Accumulation, and Extraction" *Big Data and Society* (January–June 2019): 1–12.

22. For a review of the linkage of trauma to resilience techniques and neoliberal human capital theory, see, for example, Paul Tough, *How Children Succeed: Grit, Curiosity and the Hidden Power of Character* (New York: Houghton-Mifflin, 2012). Angela Duckworth and James Heckman are key academic figures in making these connections. I discussed this specifically with regard to grit pedagogy in "The Austerity School: Grit, Character, and the Privatization of Public Education," in Saltman, *Scripted Bodies.*

23. Saltman, "The Austerity School."

24. Heather Roberts-Mahoney, Mark Garrison, and Alexander Means, "Netflixing Human Capital Development: Personalized Learning Technology and the Corporatization of K-12 Education," *Journal of Education Policy* 31, no. 4 (2016): 405–420.

25. Natasha Singer, "The Silicon Valley Billionaires Remaking America's Schools," *New York Times*, June 6, 2017.

26. Singer, "The Silicon Valley Billionaires Remaking America's Schools."

27. See the IMOTIONS website: https://imotions.com/education -communication/. I discuss the Affdex biometric pedagogy technology and its assumptions about the process of teaching, learning, and knowledge in Saltman, *Scripted Bodies*. For an analysis of how Affdex represents a project of objectivizing affect and behavior, see Williamson and Piattoeva, "Objectivity as Standardization in Data-Scientific Education Policy."

28. Saltman, *Scripted Bodies*.

29. Alexander J. Means, *Schooling in the Age of Austerity* (New York: Palgrave Macmillan, 2013).

30. Saltman, *Scripted Bodies,* chapter 2: "The Austerity School."

31. Williamson and Piattoeva, "Objectivity as Standardization in Data-Scientific Education Policy."

32. Williamson and Piattoeva, "Objectivity as Standardization in Data-Scientific Education Policy," 9–11.

33. Williamson and Piattoeva, "Objectivity as Standardization in Data-Scientific Education Policy," 4, 18.

34. See World Economic Forum, "Schools of the Future," 11, 13, 26.

35. Williamson and Piattoeva, "Objectivity as Standardization in Data-Scientific Education Policy," 14; Saltman, *Scripted Bodies*.

36. See Alysson McDowell's blog "Wrench in the Gears." https:// wrenchinthegears.

37. World Economic Forum, "Schools of the Future," 7.

38. World Economic Forum, "Schools of the Future," 4.

39. Henry A. Giroux, *On Critical Pedagogy*, second edition (New York: Bloomsbury, 2020).

40. World Economic Forum, "Schools of the Future," 10. The perspective of the World Economic Forum contrasts with critical pedagogy. See for example, Giroux, *On Critical Pedagogy*.

41. Paulo Freire, *Pedagogy of the Oppressed* (New York: Continuum, 1970); Donaldo Macedo, *Literacies of Power* (New York: Westview, 2006).

42. World Economic Forum, "Schools of the Future," 9.

43. Melissa Sanchez, "Investors Earn Max Initial Payment from Chicago's Social Impact Bond," *Chicago Reporter*, May 16, 2016.

44. See Gary Miron and Jessica Urschel, "A Study of Student Characteristics, School Finance and School Performance in Schools Operated by K12, Inc." National Education Policy Center (July 2012). https://nepc.colorado.edu/publication/understanding-improving-virtual.

45. For example, see Hess, Manno, and Meeks, "From School Choice to Educational Choice."

46. Sadowski, "When Datafication Is Capital."

47. Emma Brown and Todd C. Frankel, "Facebook Backed School Software Shows Promise and Raises Privacy Concerns," *Washington Post*, October 11, 2016. https://www.washingtonpost.com/local/education/facebook-backed-school-software-shows-promise-and-raises-privacy-concerns/2016/10/11/2580f9fe-80c6-11e6-b002-307601806392_story.html.

48. Faith Boninger, Alex Molnar, and Christopher Saldana, "Personalized Learning and the Digital Privatization of Curriculum and Teaching," National Education Policy Center (April 2019). https://nepc.colorado.edu/publication/personalized-learning.

49. See https://www.newschools.org/.

50. For the continuity from venture philanthropy promoting charter-based privatization to the newer shift to digital privatization, see the website of the NSVF: https://www.newschools.org/about-us/our-model/. I criticize the venture philanthropy agenda of privatization,

managerialism, highjacking of public governance, and use of public money for private and market-based agendas in education in Kenneth J. Saltman, *The Gift of Education: Public Education and Venture Philanthropy* (New York: Palgrave Macmillan, 2010).

51. https://www.centervention.com/social-skills-game/.

52. https://www.centervention.com/social-skills-game/.

53. Fordham Center on Law and Information Policy, "Transparency and the Marketplace for Student Data," 2018. https://www.fordham .edu/info/23830/research/10517/transparency_and_the_marketplace_ for_student_data/1; Boninger, Molnar, and Saldana, "Personalized Learning and the Digital Privatization of Curriculum and Teaching."

54. World Economic Forum, "Schools of the Future," 8.

55. Saltman, *Scripted Bodies*.

56. Robinson, *Into the Tempest*.

57. Samuel Bowles and Herbert Gintis, *Schooling in Capitalist America* (Chicago: Haymarket, 2011) (original publication in 1976); Henry A. Giroux, *Theory and Resistance in Education* (Westport, CT: Bergin & Garvey, 1983).

58. Nancy Fraser, "From Discipline to Flexibilization? Rereading Foucault in the Shadow of Globalization," *Constellations* 10, no. 2 (2003): 160–171.

59. Chapter 2 concludes with such an example of critical cultural pedagogy (the video art installation Triple Chaser) in which Forensic Architecture used AI to illuminate concealed power relationships and the ties between states, corporations, and cultural institutions. Another example that more explicitly references critical pedagogy and also was conducted in an informal educational setting was Annette Markham's Museum of Random Memory project, which is an interactive experience in which visitors are "memory donors" collectively building a memory archive. The different parts of the moving exhibit aim to teach participants how memory is changed as it is digitalized. The project uses digital tracking software to teach participants about digital surveillance and to foster data literacy. Although this project

admirably and creatively develops participant interaction that raises questions about the uses and social effects of technology, it does not connect the cultural politics of memory and technology to a political economic engagement with the dimensions of memory and technology. It could be developed to do so. See Annette N. Markham, "Taking Data Literacy to the Streets: Critical Pedagogy in the Public Sphere," *Qualitative Inquiry* 26(2), 227–237.

CHAPTER 4

1. Rachel Parker and Bo Stjerne Thomsen, "Executive Summary: Learning through Play at School," White Paper LEGO Foundation (March 2019), 1, 9.

2. Diane Levin makes this argument in the documentary *Mickey Mouse Monopoly* (2002), produced by Media Education Foundation. It can be found in the transcript on page 17. Transcript available at https://www.mediaed.org/transcripts/Mickey-Mouse-Monopoly-Transcript.pdf.

3. This school commercialism criticism can be seen as naive in the sense that childrens' narratives are greatly informed by ideologies that circulate in cultures. In this sense, the LEGO project of supplying children with premade corporate narrative derived from Hollywood movies and mass marketed video games ought to be scrutinized not only for providing prefabricated stories but also for the kinds of ideologies, values, and identifications supplied to children that form the building blocks of their narratives and play. Such largely conservatizing commercial ideologies need to be understood in contrast to other, more emancipatory ideologies, values, and identifications that accord with broader ethical and political values of equality, democracy, and justice. See Henry A. Giroux, *The Mouse That Roared: Disney and the End of Innocence* (Lanham, MD: Rowman & Littlefield, 1999).

4. The LEGO Foundation's reports and advocacy materials make these aims explicit, and the OECD's reports include the play-based learning agenda as part of its neoliberal human capital development perspective. See, for example, Rachel Parker and Bo Stjerne Thomsen, "Executive Summary: Learning through Play at School," White Paper LEGO Foundation (March 2019); Ben Mardell, Daniel Wilson, Jen Ryan, Katie Ertel, Mara Drechevsky, and Megina Baker, "Towards a Pedagogy of Play: A Project

Zero Working Paper" (July 2016); The LEGO Foundation, "Assessing Creativity: A Palette of Possibilities," https://www.legofoundation.com/en/learn-how/knowledge-base/assessing-creativity/; The Pedagogy of Play Research Team, "Playful Participatory Research: An Emerging Methodology for Developing a Pedagogy of Play," a Project Zero Working Paper [Project Zero at Harvard Graduate School of Education/International School at Billund Funded by LEGO Foundation] (July 2016); The LEGO Foundation, "What We Mean by Creativity," 2 [a leaflet]; The LEGO Foundation, "Creating Systems: How Can Education Systems Reform to Enhance Learners' Creativity?" Creativity Matters no. 2, https://www.legofoundation.com/en/why-play/skills-for-holistic-development/creativity-matters/creativity-matters-report-series/creating-systems/; Bonnie Cramond, "Appendix: Choosing a Creativity Assessment That Is Fit for Purpose," The LEGO Foundation, https://www.legofoundation.com/media/2345/appendix_assessingcreativity_pdf.pdf.

5. On the discourse of childhood innocence and its political and pedagogical dimensions, see Giroux, *The Mouse That Roared,* and Henry A. Giroux, *Stealing Innocence: Youth, Corporate Power, and the Politics of Culture* (New York: Palgrave Macmillan, 2000).

6. Robin Truth Goodman, personal communication.

7. James Vaznis, "Schools Are Collecting New Data in New Ways about Students with Cutting-Edge High-Tech," *Boston Globe,* December 16, 2019. https://www.bostonglobe.com/metro/2019/12/16/schools-experiment-with-high-tech-student-monitoring/7sx3eMEqYTwO9zxzKjyEkK/story.html.

8. See Alexander J. Means, *Learning to Save the Future* (New York: Routledge, 2018). See also Nick Dyer-Witheford, Atle Mikkola Kjosen, and James Steinhoff, *Inhuman Power: Artificial Intelligence and the Future of Capitalism* (London: Pluto Press, 2019).

9. Jeff Bryant, "How Corporations Are Forcing Their Way into Public Schools," *Salon.com,* February 11, 2020. https://www.salon.com/2020/02/11/how-corporations-are-forcing-their-way-into-americas-public-schools_partner/.

10. Dorothy Shipps, *School Reform, Corporate Style: Chicago 1880–2000* (Lawrence: University of Kansas Press, 2006); Joel Spring, *Economization of Education* (New York: Routledge, 2015).

11. See Williamson and Piatteova's important discussion of the objectivization of knowledge made by supranational actors in Ben Williamson and Nelli Piattoeva, "Objectivity as Standardization in Data-Scientific Education Policy, Technology and Governance" [author's pre-publication version of article], https://www.pure.ed.ac.uk/ws/files /78326060/WilliamsonB_2018_LMT_Objectivity_standardization.pdf. Where I respectfully differ with these scholars is that they rely on a somewhat depoliticized theory of knowledge transferability to explain the allure of objectivized and quantifiable knowledge. Following Adorno, I see the draw of objectivization as a promise of concreteness in a world rendered abstract through the principle of exchange universalized and the ideology of positivism that succeeds for this reason. The key issue is that material and symbolic interests and ideologies drive knowledge formation practices, and the objectivization is part of a hegemonic project of ruling blocs to universalize their partial, class-, and group-specific knowledge. I draw on their important scholarship and discuss my differences with Williamson and Piatteova at greater length in chapter 6.

12. Parker and Thomsen, "Executive Summary: Learning through Play at School"; Mardell et al., "Towards a Pedagogy of Play"; The LEGO Foundation, "Assessing Creativity"; The Pedagogy of Play Research Team, "Playful Participatory Research"; The LEGO Foundation, "What We Mean by Creativity," 2; The LEGO Foundation, "Creating Systems"; Cramond, "Appendix: Choosing a Creativity Assessment That Is Fit for Purpose."

13. See Ollie Bray, "How Playful Interventions Can Support High Quality Learning in Schools," Learn How blog, The LEGO Foundation, June 28, 2019. https://www.legofoundation.com/en/learn-how/blog/how-playful -interventions-can-support-high-quality-learning-in-schools/. See the Creativity Matters section of the LEGO Foundation website, https:// www.legofoundation.com/en/why-play/skills-for-holistic-development /creativity-matters/, which includes a series of reports.

   See also OECD, "Social and Emotional Skills: Well-Being, Connectedness, and Success," Paris: OECD; World Economic Forum, "Schools of the Future: Defining New Models of Education for the Fourth Industrial Revolution," January 2020, 1–33, https://www.weforum.org. Parker and Thomsen, "Executive Summary: Learning through Play at

School"; Mandell et al., "Towards a Pedagogy of Play"; The LEGO Foundation, "Assessing Creativity"; The Pedagogy of Play Research Team, "Playful Participatory Research"; The LEGO Foundation, "What We Mean by Creativity," 2; The LEGO Foundation, "Creating Systems"; Cramond, "Appendix: Choosing a Creativity Assessment That Is Fit For Purpose."

14. The three main projects of the LEGO Foundation's "Focus Geographies: Early Childhood and Education" are available at https://www .legofoundation.com.

15. See for example, Parker and Thomsen, "Learning through Play at School," 1.

16. Parker and Thomsen, "Learning through Play at School," 2.

17. Parker and Thomsen, "Learning through Play at School," 4.

18. Mandell et al., "Towards a Pedagogy of Play," 9.

19. Parker and Thomsen, "Executive Summary," 7.

20. Parker and Thomsen, "Executive Summary," 7; Ben Mardell, Daniel Wilson, Jen Ryan, Katie Ertel, Mara Drechevsky, and Megina Baker, "Towards a Pedagogy of Play: A Project Zero Working Paper" (July 2016), 6.

21. Parker and Thomsen, "Executive Summary," 12.

22. Mardell, "Towards a Pedagogy," 11.

23. Mardell, "Towards a Pedagogy," 12: "the cultivation of playful dispositions will enable them to be creative and collaborative contributors to the world's challenges. These playful dispositions are needed not just in Tue's school but around the world. A pedagogy of play will help us look to the future by providing a framework, tools, and pictures of practice to better understand, document, and support playful learning for all children."

24. The Pedagogy of Play Research Team, "Playful Participatory Research," 3.

25. The LEGO Foundation, "Assessing Creativity," 4.

26. Elizabeth McLure, "Introduction," *Assessing Creativity: A Palette of Possibilities* LEGO Foundation, 6.

27. The LEGO Foundation, "What We Mean by Creativity," 2.

28. The LEGO Foundation, "What We Mean by Creativity," 5.

29. The LEGO Foundation, "What We Mean by Creativity," 6.

30. The LEGO Foundation, "What We Mean by Creativity," 7.

31. The LEGO Foundation, "What We Mean by Creativity," 8.

32. Gregory Schmidt, "Lego Builds an Empire Brick by Brick," *New York Times*, February 14, 2014.

CHAPTER 5

1. CRASSH News. "Brexit and Trump Voters More Likely to Believe in Conspiracy Theories, Survey Shows," Centre for Research in the Arts, Social Sciences and Humanities, University of Cambridge. http://www.crassh.cam.ac.uk/blog/post/brexit-and-trump-voters-more-likely-to-believe-in-conspiracy-theories-surve.

2. Evans, Richard J. "Conspiracy Theories and Anti-Semitism," presentation to the All-Party Parliamentary Group against Antisemitism. Palace of Westminster, June 19, 2018. Posted on the Conspiracy Theories website on June 22, 2018, by Conspiracy Democracy. http://www.conspiracyanddemocracy.org/www.conspiracyanddemocracy.org/blog/conspiracy-theories-and-antisemitism/index.html.

3. Viren Swami and Rebecca Coles, "The Truth Is Out There," *The Psychologist* 23, no.7 (July 2010): 561. www.thepsychologist.org.uk.

4. See Evans, "Conspiracy Theories and Anti-Semitism."

5. Hugo Drochon's opinion piece offering advice for combating conspiracy theories is grounded in his collaborative research from the 5-year Cambridge University study. See Hugo Drochon, "Britains Are Swallowing Conspiracy Theory: Here's How to Stop the Rot," *The Guardian*, November 28, 2018. https://www.theguardian.com/commentisfree/2018/nov/28/britons-swallowing-conspiracy-theories-stop-rot-research-fake-news.

6. Jason Stanley, *How Fascism Works: The Politics of Us and Them* (New York: Random House, 2018).

7. Fact Checker, *Washington Post*, September 11, 2020. https://www
.washingtonpost.com/graphics/politics/trump-claims-database
/?itid=lk_inline_manual_3.

8. Martin Gilens and Benjamin Page, "Testing Theories of American
Politics: Elites, Interest Groups, and Average Citizens," *Perspectives on
Politics* 12, no. 3 (September 2014): 564–581.

9. See David Hursh, *High-Stakes Testing and the Decline of Teaching and
Learning* (Lanham, MD: Rowman & Littlefield, 2008); Mark Garrison,
A Measure of Failure: The Political Origins of Standardized Testing (Albany,
NY: SUNY Press, 2009); Henry A. Giroux, *Education and the Crisis of
Public Values* (New York: Peter Lang, 2013). See also Stephanie Simon,
"No Profit Left Behind," *Politico*, February 10, 2015. https://www
.politico.com/story/2015/02/pearson-education-115026; Jake Jacobs,
"Biden Is Reigniting the Movement to Oppose Standardized Testing,"
The Progressive, March 22, 2021. https://progressive.org/public-schools
-advocate/biden-movement-oppose-standardized-test-jacobs-210322/.

10. See, for example, Theodor Adorno, *Lectures on Negative Dialectics,* ed.
Rolf Tiedemann, trans. Rodney Livingstone (Malden, MA: Polity, 2008),
and Theodor Adorno, *Introduction to Sociology,* ed. Christoph Gödde,
trans. Edmund Jephcott (Stanford, CA: Stanford University Press, 2000).

11. Adorno, *Introduction to Sociology.*

12. Theodor Adorno, *History and Freedom: Lectures 1964–1965,* ed. Rolf
Tiedmann, trans. Rodney Livingstone (Malden, MA: Polity, 2008).

13. Hubert Dreyfuss, *On the Internet* (New York: Routledge, 2010).

14. Henry A. Giroux's *Theory and Resistance in Education* (Westport, CT:
Bergin & Garvey, 1983) both draws on the Frankfurt School criticism
of positivism to analyze public education and challenges deterministic
readings of the implication of positivism in social and cultural reproduction that delimit agency and political possibilities. Even as the
uses of positivism have evolved, Giroux's discussion remains highly
relevant for positioning critical pedagogy against positivism, particularly in the ongoing and new iterations of educational privatization.
See also Henry A. Giroux, "Schooling and the Culture of Positivism,"
Educational Theory 29, no. 4 (1979): 263–284.

15. Heather Roberts-Mahoney, Alexander Means, and Mark Garrison "Netflixing Human Capital Development: Personalized Learning Technology and the Corporatization of K–12 Education," *Journal of Education Policy* 31, no. 4 (2016): 405–420.

16. I discuss adaptive learning technology by examining the Chan Zuckerberg Initiative's Summit in Kenneth J. Saltman, *The Swindle of Innovative Educational Finance* (Minneapolis: University of Minnesota Press, 2018).

17. Adorno, *Introduction to Sociology,* 32.

18. Karl Popper, "Towards a Rational Theory of Tradition," chapter 4 in *Conjectures and Refutations: The Growth of Scientific Knowledge,* second ed. (New York: Routledge 2002), 165–168.

19. Adorno, *Introduction to Sociology,* 22–25. The quote is from page 19. Adorno continues: "For on the other hand these laws contain the possibility, the potential, that all will be different, that society will stop being the coercive union in which we find ourselves. But these objective laws are valid only to [the] extent that they express themselves in social phenomena, and not if they are no more than a mere deduction from pure concepts, however deeply such deductions may be rooted in social knowledge" (page 22).

20. Adorno, *Introduction to Sociology,* 75.

CHAPTER 6

1. Kim Parker, "The Growing Partisan Divide in Views of Higher Education," Pew Research Center, January 30, 2019. https://www .pewresearch.org/social-trends/2019/08/19/the-growing-partisan -divide-in-views-of-higher-education-2/.

2. Cary Funk, Brian Kennedy, and Courtney Johnson, "Trust in Medical Scientists Has Grown in U.S., but Mainly among Democrats," Pew Research Center, May 21, 2020. https://www.pewresearch.org/science /2020/05/21/trust-in-medical-scientists-has-grown-in-u-s-but-mainly -among-democrats/.

3. Kaitlyn Tiffany, "How a Conspiracy Theory about Democrats Drinking Children's Blood Topped Amazon's Best-Sellers List," *Vox,*

March 6, 2019. https://www.vox.com/the-goods/2019/3/6/18253505 /amazon-qanon-book-best-seller-algorithm-conspiracy.

4. Ari Drennen and Sally Hardin, "Climate Deniers in the 117th Congress," Center for American Progress. https://www.americanprogress .org/issues/green/news/2021/03/30/497685/climate-deniers-117th -congress/.

5. Theodore M. Porter, *Trust in Numbers: The Pursuit of Objectivity in Science and Public Life* (Princeton, NJ: Princeton University Press, 1995), viii.

6. Porter, *Trust in Numbers,* ix.

7. Porter, *Trust in Numbers,* 8.

8. Porter, *Trust in Numbers,* 8 and 77.

9. Porter, *Trust in Numbers,* 5.

10. Porter, *Trust in Numbers,* 7.

11. Sander van der Linden, Costas Panagopoulos, Flavio Azevedo, and John T. Jost, "The Paranoid Style in American Politics Revisited: An Ideological Asymmetry in Conspiratorial Thinking," *Political Psychology* 42, no. 1 (2021): 23–51.

12. William I. Robinson, *The Global Police State* (London: Pluto Press, 2020).

13. In particular, see Nancy Fraser, *The Old Is Dying and the New Cannot Be Born* (London: Verso, 2019); Robinson, *The Global Police State.*

14. On the crises facing education and agency, see Henry A. Giroux, "Does Critical Pedagogy Have a Future?" in *On Critical Pedagogy* (New York: Bloomsbury, 2011), 171. On the evisceration of investigative journalism and the expansion of advertising and public relations content, see Robert W. McChesney, *Digital Disconnect: How Capitalism Is Turning the Internet against Democracy* (New York: The New Press, 2013).

15. Martin Gilens and Benjamin Page, "Testing Theories of American Politics: Elites, Interest Groups, and Average Citizens," *Perspectives on Politics* 12, no. 3 (September 2014): 564–581.

16. Henry A. Giroux, "A Critical Interview with Henry Giroux," *Global Education Magazine*, January 30, 2013. https://www.globaleducation magazine.com/critical-interview-henry-giroux/.

17. Kenneth J. Saltman and David Gabbard, eds., *Education as Enforcement: The Militarization and Corporatization of Schools* (New York: Routledge, 2010); Giroux, *On Critical Pedagogy*; David Hursh, *High-Stakes Testing and the Decline of Teaching and Learning* (Lanham, MD: Rowman & Littlefield, 2008).

18. McChesney, *Digital Disconnect.*

19. Robinson, *The Global Police State.*

20. Giroux, *On Critical Pedagogy,* 171.

21. Jeremy Barr, "Critical Race Theory Was the Hot Topic on Fox News This Summer. Not So Much Any More," *Washington Post,* October 6, 2021.

22. Richard Hofstadter, "The Paranoid Style in American Politics," *Harper's Magazine,* November 1964.

23. Jason Stanley, *How Fascism Works: The Politics of Us and Them* (New York: Random House, 2018).

24. Porter, *Trust in Numbers,* 3.

25. Porter, *Trust in Numbers,* 7; see Lorraine Daston and Peter Galison, *Objectivity* (New York: Zone Books, 2007).

26. Chantal Mouffe, *The Return of the Political* (New York: Verso, 1992); Chantal Mouffe, *For a Left Populism* (New York: Verso, 2018).

27. Mouffe, *The Return of the Political.*

28. Mouffe, *For a Left Populism,* 24.

29. These fabulist conspiracy narratives about children remain silent about the real quotidien exploitation and abuse of children by capital through commercialism; the state-sponsored abuse of migrant children at the border; the torture of children in the Global War on Terrorism; and the grotesque levels of homelessness, poverty, and public and private disinvestment in services experienced by millions of US children every day. These conspiracy narratives trade in the discourse of childhood innocence and mimic longstanding scapegoating

narratives, such as the blood libel against Jews, while sometimes intersecting with revived anti-Semitism through coded tropes about cabals of "globalist" elites.

30. Robinson, *The Global Police State*, 131.

31. CASEL website at https://casel.org.

32. Ben Williamson and Nelli Piattoeva, "Objectivity as Standardization in Data-Scientific Education Policy, Technology and Governance" [authors' pre-publication version], (2018), 2–3. https://www.pure.ed.ac.uk/ws/files/78326060/WilliamsonB_2018_LMT_Objectivity_standardization.pdf.

33. Williamson and Piattoeva, 5.

34. Williamson and Piattoeva, 5.

35. Williamson and Piattoeva, 5.

36. Robin Truth Goodman, personal communication, May 10, 2021.

37. I discuss the cultural politics of biometric pedagogy in Kenneth J. Saltman, *Scripted Bodies: Corporate Power, Smart Technologies, and the Undoing of Public Education* (New York: Routledge, 2016), and that of adaptive learning technology in Kenneth J. Saltman, *The Swindle of Innovative Educational Finance* (Minneapolis: University of Minnesota Press, 2018).

38. Jathan Sadowski, "When Data Is Capital: Datafication, Accumulation, and Extraction," *Big Data and Society,* January 7, 2019.

39. Heather Roberts-Mahoney, Alexander Means, and Mark Garrison. "Netflixing Human Capital Development: Personalized Learning Technology in the Corporatization of K–12 Education," *Journal of Education Policy* 31, no. 4 (2016): 1–16.

40. Faith Boninger, Alex Molnar, and C. Saldana, "Personalized Learning and the Digital Privatization of Curriculum and Teaching," National Education Policy Center (April 2019), 10. http://nepc.colorado.edu/publication/personalized-learning.

41. James Vaznis, "Schools Are Collecting New Data in New Ways about Students with Cutting-Edge High Tech," *Boston Globe*, December 16, 2019. https://www.bostonglobe.com/metro/2019/12/16/schools-experiment

-with-high-tech-student-monitoring/7sx3eMEqYTwO9zxzKjyEkK/story
.html.

42. See Astra Taylor, "The Automation Charade," *Logic,* August 1, 2018. https://logicmag.io/failure/the-automation-charade/.

43. Erich Fromm, "Paranoia and Policy," *New York Times,* December 11, 1975.

44. See, for example, the film directed by Sut Jhally, *Race: The Floating Signifier* (Northampton, MA: Media Education Foundation, 1997).

CHAPTER 7

1. On the neoliberal evacuation of the concept of the public, see Zygmunt Bauman, *In Search of Politics* (London: Polity, 1999), and Henry A. Giroux, *Public Spaces, Private Lives* (Lanham, MD: Rowman & Littlefield, 2001).

2. Asad Haider, *Mistaken Identity: Race and Class in the Age of Trump* (New York: Verso, 2018), provides a valuable criticism of how collective and structural criticisms of "white skin priviledge" were transformed into white privilege as an individual problem by, for example, Peggy MacIntosh, "White Privilege: Unpacking the Invisible Knapsack" *Peace and Freedom* July/August 1989. See Haider, *Mistaken Identity,* 46–47.

3. Angela Nagle, *Kill All Normies* (London: Zero Books, 2017).

4. Phoebe Maltz Bovy, "Checking Privilege Checking" *The Atlantic* May 7, 2014. https://www.theatlantic.com/politics/archive/2014/05 /check-your-check-your-privilege/361898/.

5. Henry A. Giroux, *Channel Surfing: Race Talk and the Destruction of Today's Youth* (New York: Palgrave Macmillan, 1997); Joe L. Kincheloe, Shirley Steinberg, Nelson Rodriguez, Ronald Chennault, White Reign: Deploying Whiteness in America (New York: St. Martin's Griffin, 2000); Ruth Frankenberg, White Women, Race Matters: The Social Construction of Whiteness (Minneapolis: University of Minnesota Press, 1993).

6. David Roediger, *Towards the Abolition of Whiteness* (New York: Verso, 1994).

7. Henry A. Giroux, *Channel Surfing: Race Talk and the Destruction of Today's Youth* (New York: Palgrave Macmillan, 1997).

8. Haider, *Mistaken Identity,* 9–10, 17. See also Michelle Alexander, *The New Jim Crow: Mass Incarceration in the Age of Colorblindness* (New York: The New Press, 2010).

9. Paul Blest, "Tucker Carlson Wants Body Cameras for Teachers to Stop Critical Race Theory," *Vice News,* July 7, 2021.

10. Robin DiAngelo, *White Fragility: Why It's So Hard for White People to Talk about Racism* (Boston: Beacon, 2018).

11. Keeanga-Yamahta Taylor, *From #Blacklivesmatter to Black Liberation* (Chicago: Haymarket, 2016), 215. Taylor's work provides a valuable antidote to the tendencies criticized here.

12. The symbolic violence of normative culture can be traumatic. Critical pedagogy takes subjective experience, including trauma, seriously in relation to the social forces that produce that experience. In turn, it suggests that the experience can be reconceptualized to become the basis for agency to impact the forces that produce the experience.

13. Theodor Adorno, *Introduction to Sociology,* ed. Christoph Gödde, trans. Edmund Jephcott (Stanford, CA: Stanford University Press, 2000).

14. I take up this trend in Kenneth J. Saltman, *Scripted Bodies: Corporate Power, Smart Technologies, and the Undoing of Public Education* (New York: Routledge, 2016).

15. To be clear, I am not endorsing university administrators inviting or defending students who invite Charles Murray to speak on campus. Murray represents a form of hate speech cloaked in bogus pseudoscience. His project of locating the intellectual limits of racial subjects in biology is at odds with any conception of democratic community and its formation through free exchange. His defense of this project should be contested and interrupted, as students did when he spoke at Middlebury College in 2017. The empirical bases of Murray's claims about racial superiority have been debunked, and the pursuit of the question he asks is not worthwhile. Murray's views and the questions

he pursues are unworthy of academic discourse. But those who would physically attack such a speaker make the mistake of grounding the speaker's position in his physical existence. This error inadvertently repeats a crucial aspect of what is wrong with Murray's position, which aims to locate intellectual limits in the essence of the body.

CONCLUSION

1. Theodor Adorno, *Introduction to Sociology,* ed. Christoph Gödde, trans. Edmund Jephcott (Stanford, CA: Stanford University Press, 2000), p. 49.

BIBLIOGRAPHY

Adorno, Theodor. *Introduction to Sociology*. Edited by Christoph Gödde, translated by Edmund Jephcott. Stanford, CA: Stanford University Press, 2000.

Adorno, Theodor. *Lectures on Negative Dialectics*. Edited by Rolf Tiedemann, translated by Rodney Livingstone. Malden, MA: Polity, 2008.

Adorno, Theodor. *History and Freedom: Lectures 1964–1965*. Edited by Rolf Tiedmann, translated by Rodney Livingstone. Malden, MA: Polity, 2008.

Alexander, Michelle. *The New Jim Crow: Mass Incarceration in the Age of Colorblindness*. New York: The New Press, 2010.

Baker, Bruce. "Picture Post Week: Subprime Chartering" (blog). School Finance 101, December 10, 2015. https://schoolfinance101.wordpress.com/2015/12/10/picture-post-week-subprime-chartering/.

Barshay, Jill. "Impact Funds Pour Money into Ed Tech Businesses." *Hechinger Report*, October 21, 2019.

Bauman, Zygmunt. *In Search of Politics*. London: Polity, 1999.

Bauman, Zygmunt. *Strangers at Our Door*. Malden, MA: Polity, 2016.

Berliner, David, and Bruce Biddle. *The Manufactured Crisis*. New York: Basic Books, 1996.

Boninger, Faith, Alex Molnar, and Kevin Murray. "Asleep at the Switch: Schoolhouse Commercialism, Student Privacy, and the Failure of

Policymaking." *National Education Policy Center,* August 2017. http://
nepc.colorado.edu/publication/schoolhouse-commercialism-2017.

Boninger, Faith, Alex Molnar, and Christopher Saldana. "Personalized Learning and the Digital Privatization of Curriculum and Teaching." National Education Policy Center, April 30, 2019. https://nepc
.colorado.edu/publication/personalized-learning.

Boser, Ulrich. "Betsy DeVos Has Invested Millions in This Brain Training Center. So I Checked It Out." *Washington Post,* May 26, 2017.
https://www.washingtonpost.com/posteverything/wp/2017/05/26
/betsy-devos-neurocore/?utm_term=.366a865e3c3d.

Bourdieu, Pierre. "The Forms of Capital." In *Handbook of Theory and
Research for the Sociology of Education.* Edited by J. Richardson. New
York: Greenwood, 1986, 241–258.

Bourdieu, Pierre, and Jean Passeron. *Reproduction in Education Society
and Culture.* Thousand Oaks, CA: Sage, 1990.

Bovy, Phoebe Maltz. "Checking Privilege Checking." *The Atlantic,* May
7, 2014. https://www.theatlantic.com/politics/archive/2014/05/check
-your-check-your-privilege/361898/.

Bowles, Samuel, and Herbert Gintis. *Schooling in Capitalist America.*
Chicago: Haymarket Books, 2011.

Bray, Ollie. "How Playful Interventions Can Support High Quality
Learning in Schools" (blog). Learn How (The LEGO Foundation), June
28, 2019. https://www.legofoundation.com/en/learn-how/blog/how
-playful-interventions-can-support-high-quality-learning-in-schools/.

Brown, Emma, and Todd C. Frankel. "Facebook Backed School Software Shows Promise and Raises Privacy Concerns." *Washington Post,*
October 11, 2016. https://www.washingtonpost.com/local/education
/facebook-backed-school-software-shows-promise-and-raises-privacy
-concerns/2016/10/11/2580f9fe-80c6-11e6-b002-307601806392
_story.html.

Bryant, Jake, and Jimmy Sarakatsannis. "Why US Education Is Ready
for Investment." McKinsey & Company, July 2015. https://www
.mckinsey.com/industries/education/our-insights/why-us-education
-is-ready-for-investment.

Bryant, Jeff. "How Corporations Are Forcing Their Way into Public Schools." Salon.com, February 11, 2020. https://www.salon.com/2020/02/11/how-corporations-are-forcing-their-way-into-americas-public-schools_partner/.

Carnoy, Martin. "School Vouchers Are Not a Proven Strategy for Improving Student Achievement." Economic Policy Institute, February 28, 2017. http://www.epi.org/publication/school-vouchers-are-not-a-proven-strategy-for-improving-student-achievement/.

CASEL website. https://casel.org.

Chakraborty, Sayan. "BYJU's Updates App, Aims to Make Profits This Year." LiveMint, May 24, 2017. https://www.livemint.com/Companies/W0pmP4tPipqmo8ozq9lMDJ/Byjus-updates-app-aims-to-make-profits-this-year.html.

Chomsky, Noam, and Marv Waterstone. *Consequences of Capitalism: Manufacturing Discontent and Resistance.* Chicago: Haymarket Books, 2021.

Clark, Jocalyn, and Linsey McGoey. "The Black Box Warning on Philanthrocapitalism." *The Lancet* 388 (2016): 2457–2459.

Couldry, Nick, and Ulises A Meijas. *The Costs of Connection: How Data Is Colonizing Human Life and Appropriating It for Capitalism.* Stanford, CA: Stanford University Press, 2019.

Cramond, Bonnie. "Appendix: Choosing a Creativity Assessment That Is Fit for Purpose." The LEGO Foundation. Retrieved July 23, 2021. https://www.legofoundation.com/media/2345/appendix_assessing creativity_pdf.pdf.

CRASSH News. "Brexit and Trump Voters More Likely to Believe in Conspiracy Theories, Survey Shows." Centre for Research in the Arts, Social Sciences and Humanities, University of Cambridge, November 23, 2018. http://www.crassh.cam.ac.uk/blog/post/brexit-and-trump-voters-more-likely-to-believe-in-conspiracy-theories-surve.

Daston, Lorraine, and Peter Galison. *Objectivity.* New York: Zone Books, 2007.

Drennen, Ari, and Sally Hardin. "Climate Deniers in the 117th Congress." *Center for American Progress*, March 30, 2021. https://www

.americanprogress.org/issues/green/news/2021/03/30/497685/climate
-deniers-117th-congress/.

Dreyfuss, Hubert. *On the Internet.* New York: Routledge, 2010.

Drochon, Hugo. "Britains Are Swallowing Conspiracy Theory: Here's
How to Stop the Rot." *The Guardian*, November 28, 2018. https://www
.theguardian.com/commentisfree/2018/nov/28/britons-swallowing
-conspiracy-theories-stop-rot-research-fake-news.

Dyer-Witheford, Nick, Atle Mikkola Kjosen, and James Steinhoff. *Inhuman Power: Artificial Intelligence and the Future of Capitalism.* London:
Pluto Press, 2019.

Dykes, Daniel, and Michael S. Schwartz. "The Chan Zuckerberg Initiative." *Trusts and Estates,* May 2016.

Emma, Caitlin, Benjamin Wermund, and Kimberly Hefling. "DeVos'
Michigan Schools Experiment Gets Poor Grades." *Politico*, December 9,
2016. http://www.politico.com/story/2016/12/betsy-devos-michigan
-school-experiment-232399.

Eubanks, Virginia. *Automating Inequality.* New York: St. Martin's Press,
2017.

Evans, Richard J. "Conspiracy Theories and Anti-Semitism." Presentation to the All-Party Parliamentary Group against Antisemitism. Palace of Westminster, June 19, 2018. Posted in Conspiracy
Theories on June 22, 2018, by Conspiracy Democracy. http://www
.conspiracyanddemocracy.org/www.conspiracyanddemocracy.org
/blog/conspiracy-theories-and-antisemitism/index.html.

Executive Office of the President, National Science and Technology
Council Committee on Technology White House Report. "Preparing for the Future of Artificial Intelligence," May 2014. https://
obamawhitehouse.archives.gov/sites/default/files/whitehouse_files
/microsites/ostp/NSTC/preparing_for_the_future_of_ai.pdf.

Fact Checker. *Washington Post,* August 4, 2018. https://www.wash
ingtonpost.com/news/fact-checker/wp/2018/08/01/president-trump
-has-made-4229-false-or-misleading-claims-in-558-days/?utm_term
=.49e4aee342c8.

Fact Checker. "President Trump Has Made 12,019 False or Misleading Claims over 928 Days." *Washington Post,* August 12, 2019. https://www.washingtonpost.com/politics/2019/08/12/president-trump-has-made-false-or-misleading-claims-over-days/.

Feren, Megan. "Remote Learning and School Reopenings: What Worked and What Didn't." *Center for American Progress,* July 6, 2021. https://www.americanprogress.org/issues/education-k-12/reports/2021/07/06/501221/remote-learning-school-reopenings-worked-didnt/.

Fisher, Mark. *Capitalist Realism: Is There No Alternative?* London: Zero Books, 2009.

Fordham Center on Law and Information Policy. "Transparency and the Marketplace for Student Data," 2018. https://www.fordham.edu/info/23830/research/10517/transparency_and_the_marketplace_for_student_data/1.

Forensic Architecture Video installation artwork "Triple Chaser." Whitney Biennial. August 2019. https://forensic-architecture.org/investigation/triple-chaser.

Frankenberg, Ruth. *White Women, Race Matter: The Social Construction of Whiteness.* Minneapolis: University of Minnesota Press, 1993.

Fraser, Nancy. "From Discipline to Flexibilization? Rereading Foucault in the Shadow of Globalization." *Constellations* 10, no. 2 (2003): 160–171.

Fraser, Nancy. *The Old Is Dying and the New Cannot Be Born.* New York: Verso Books, 2019.

Fraser, Nancy. *Unruly Practices: Power, Discourse, and Gender in Contemporary Social Theory.* Minneapolis: University of Minnesota Press, 1989.

Freire, Paulo. *Pedagogy of the Oppressed.* New York: Continuum, 1970.

Freire, Paulo. *Pedagogy of the Oppressed.* New York: Continuum, 1972.

Fromm, Erich. *Escape from Freedom* (London: Routledge, Keegan & Paul, 1941).

Fromm, Erich. "Paranoia and Policy." *New York Times,* December 11, 1975.

Funk, Cary, Brian Kennedy, and Courtney Johnson. "Trust in Medical Scientists Has Grown in U.S., but Mainly among Democrats." *Pew Research Center*, May 21, 2020. https://www.pewresearch.org/science /2020/05/21/trust-in-medical-scientists-has-grown-in-u-s-but-mainly -among-democrats/.

Garrison, Mark. *A Measure of Failure: The Political Origins of Standardized Testing*. Albany, NY: SUNY Press, 2009.

Gilens, Martin, and Benjamin Page. "Testing Theories of American Politics: Elites, Interest Groups, and Average Citizens." *Perspectives on Politics* 12, no. 3 (2014): 564–581.

Giroux, Henry. "A Critical Interview with Henry Giroux." *Global Education Magazine*, January 30, 2013. https://www.globaleducation magazine.com/critical-interview-henry-giroux/.

Giroux, Henry A. *Channel Surfing: Racism, the Media, and the Destruction of Today's Youth*. New York: St. Martin's Press, 1998.

Giroux, Henry A. *Education and the Crisis of Public Values*. New York: Peter Lang, 2013.

Giroux, Henry A. *The Mouse That Roared: Disney and the End of Innocence*. Lanham, MD: Rowman & Littlefield, 1999.

Giroux, Henry A. *On Critical Pedagogy*, second edition. New York: Bloomsbury, 2020.

Giroux, Henry A. *On Critical Pedagogy*. New York: Bloomsbury, 2011.

Giroux, Henry A. *Public Spaces, Private Lives*. Lanham, MD: Rowman & Littlefield, 2001.

Giroux, Henry A. *Stealing Innocence: Youth, Corporate Power, and the Politics of Culture*. New York: Palgrave Macmillan, 2000.

Giroux, Henry A. *Theory and Resistance in Education*. Westport, CT: Bergin & Garvey, 1983.

Glass, Gene, and David Berliner. *50 Myths and Lies That Threaten America's Public Schools: The Real Crisis in Education*. New York: Teachers College Press, 2014.

Gould, Stephen Jay. *The Mismeasure of Man*. New York: Norton, 1996.

Green, Erica L. "DeVos Funnels Coronavirus Relief Funds to Favored Private and Religious Schools." *New York Times,* May 15, 2020.

Haider, Asad. *Mistaken Identity: Race and Class in the Age of Trump.* New York: Verso Books, 2018.

Hall, Stuart. *Representation: Cultural Representations and Signifying Practices.* Thousand Oaks, CA: Sage, 1997.

Harvey, David. *A Brief History of Neoliberalism.* Oxford: Oxford University Press, 2005.

Hess, Frederick, Bruno Manno, and Olivia Meeks. "From School Choice to Educational Choice." American Enterprise Institute. https://www.aei .org/research-products/report/from-school-choice-to-educational-choice/.

Hill, Paul T., Christine Campbell, David Menefee-Libey, Brianna Dusseault, , Michael DeArmond, , Betheny Gross, . "Portfolio School Districts for Big Cities: An Interim Report." *Center on Reinventing Public Education,* October 2009.

Hofstadter, Richard. "The Paranoid Style in American Politics." *Harper's Magazine,* November 1964.

Hursh, David. *High-Stakes Testing and the Decline of Teaching and Learning.* Lanham, MD: Rowman & Littlefield, 2008.

Jhally, Sut, director. *Race: The Floating Signifier.* Northampton, MA: Media Education Foundation, 1997.

Kashyap, Sindhu. "Why BYJU's Chose to Bet on Edurite and Tutorvista." *Your Story,* May 15, 2017. https://yourstory.com/2017/05/byjus -edurite-tutorvista/.

Kincheloe, Joe L., Shirley Steinberg, Nelson Rodriguez, Ronald Chennault., editors. *White Reign: Deploying Whiteness in America.* New York: St. Martin's Press, 2000.

Kipnis, Laura. *Unwanted Advances.* New York: HarperCollins, 2017.

Kliebard, Herbert. *The Struggle for the American Curriculum, 1893–1958,* third edition. New York: Routledge, 2004.

Koerth-Baker, Maggie. "Why Rational People Buy into Conspiracy Theories." *New York Times Magazine,* May 21, 2013.

Kronk, H. "Johns Hopkins Researchers Found 'Significant Problems' with Summit Learning Use in Providence Schools." *E-Learning Inside*, July 1, 2019. https://news.elearninginside.com/johns-hopkins -researchers-found-significant-problems-with-summit-learning-use-in -providence-schools/.

Leonhardt, David. "A Plea for a Fact-Based Debate about Charter Schools." *New York Times*, July 22, 2018.

Levine, Martin. "Chan Zuckerberg LLC: No Tax Breaks + No Accountability = What Exactly?" *Non-Profit Quarterly*, December 7, 2015.

Macedo, Donaldo. *Literacies of Power*. New York: Westview, 2006.

Macintosh, Peggy. "White Privilege: Unpacking the Invisible Knapsack." *Peace and Freedom Magazine*, July/August 1989, 10–12.

Manolev, Jamie, Anna Sullivan, and Roger Slee. "The Datafication of Discipline: Class Dojo, Surveillance and a Performative Classroom Culture." *Learning, Media and Technology* 44, no. 1 (2018): 36–51.

Mardell, Ben, Daniel Wilson, Jen Ryan, Katie Ertel, Mara Drechevsky, and Megina Baker. "Towards a Pedagogy of Play: A Project Zero Working Paper," July 2016. http://pz.harvard.edu/sites/default/files /Towards%20a%20Pedagogy%20of%20Play.pdf

McChesney, Robert W. *Digital Disconnect: How Capitalism Is Turning the Internet against Democracy*. New York: The New Press, 2013.

McLure, Elizabeth. "Introduction." In *Assessing Creativity: A Palette of Possibilities*. LEGO Foundation. https://cms.learningthroughplay.com /media/u1wf1xou/assessing-creativity_may2020.pdf.

McWilliams, Susan. "This Political Theorist Predicted the Rise of Trumpism: His Name Was Hunter S. Thompson." *The Nation*, December 15, 2016.

Means, Alexander J. *Learning to Save the Future*. New York: Routledge, 2018.

Means, Alexander J. *Schooling in the Age of Austerity*. New York: Palgrave Macmillan, 2014.

Mickey Mouse Monopoly. Film. (2002)

Miron, Gary, and Jessica Urschel. "A Study of Student Characteristics, School Finance and School Performance in Schools Operated by K12, Inc." National Education Policy Center, July 2012. https://nepc .colorado.edu/publication/understanding-improving-virtual.

Molnar, A. editor, G. Miron, M. K. Barbour, L. Huerta, S. R. Shafer, J. K. Rice, A. Glover, N. Browning, S. Hagle, and F. Boninger. "Virtual Schools in the U.S. 2021." Boulder: National Education Policy Center (2021). http://nepc.colorado.edu/publication/virtual-schools-annual-2021.

Mouffe, Chantal. *Agonistics: Thinking the World Politically.* New York: Verso Books, 2014.

Mouffe, Chantal. *For a Left Populism.* New York: Verso Books, 2018.

Mouffe, Chantal. *The Return of the Political.* New York: Verso Books, 1992.

Nagle, Angela. *Kill All Normies.* Alresford, UK: Zero Books, 2017.

National Assessment of Educational Progress (NAEP). "How Did U.S. Students Perform on the Most Recent Assessments?" https://www .nationsreportcard.gov/.

OECD. "Social and Emotional Skills: Well-Being, Connectedness, and Success." Paris: OECD.

O'Neil, Cathy. *Weapons of Math Destruction.* New York: Broadway Books, 2016.

Pane, J. F. "Strategies for Implementing Personalized Learning While Evidence and Resources Are Underdeveloped." Santa Monica, CA: Rand Corporation, 2018.

Parker, Kim. "The Growing Partisan Divide in Views of Higher Education." *Pew Research Center,* January 30, 2019. https://www.pewresearch .org/social-trends/2019/08/19/the-growing-partisan-divide-in-views -of-higher-education-2/.

Parker, Rachel, and Bo Stjerne Thomsen. "Executive Summary: Learning through Play at School." White Paper, LEGO Foundation, March 2019.

Popper, Karl. "Towards a Rational Theory of Tradition." In *Conjectures and Refutations: The Growth of Scientific Knowledge,* second edition. New York: Routledge, 2002, 165–168.

Porter, Theodore M. *Trust in Numbers: The Pursuit of Objectivity in Science and Public Life.* Princeton, NJ: Princeton University Press, 1995.

Reardon, Sean F., and Rebecca Hinze-Pifer. "Test Score Growth among Chicago Public School Students, 2009–2014." Stanford, CA: Stanford Center for Education Policy Analysis, November 2017.

Roberts-Mahoney, Heather, Alexander Means, and Mark Garrison. "Netflixing Human Capital Development: Personalized Learning Technology in the Corporatization of K–12 Education." *Journal of Education Policy* 31, no. 4 (2016): 1–16.

Robinson, William I. *The Global Police State.* London: Pluto Press, 2020.

Robinson, William I. *Into the Tempest: Essays on the New Global Capitalism.* Chicago: Haymarket Books, 2018.

Roediger, David. *Toward the Abolition of Whiteness.* Chicago: Haymarket Books, 1994.

Sadowski, Jathan. "When Data Is Capital: Datafication, Accumulation, and Extraction." *Big Data and Society,* January–June 2019, 1–12.

Saltman, Kenneth J. "Antitheory, Positivism, and Critical Pedagogy." In *What's Wrong with Anti-Theory.* Edited by J. R. Di Leo. New York: Bloomsbury, 2020, 73–91.

Saltman, Kenneth J. *The Failure of Corporate School Reform.* New York: Routledge, 2012.

Saltman, Kenneth J. *The Gift of Education: Public Education and Venture Philanthropy.* New York: Palgrave Macmillan, 2010.

Saltman, Kenneth J. *Scripted Bodies: Corporate Power, Smart Technologies, and the Undoing of Public Education.* New York: Routledge, 2016.

Saltman, Kenneth J. *The Swindle of Innovative Educational Finance.* Minneapolis: University of Minnesota Press, 2018.

Saltman, Kenneth J., and Alexander J. Means, editors. *The Wiley Handbook of Global Educational Reform.* Medford, MA: Wiley Blackwell, 2019.

Sanchez, Melissa. "Investors Earn Max Initial Payment from Chicago's Social Impact Bond." *Chicago Reporter,* May 16, 2016.

Schmidt, Gregory. "Lego Builds an Empire Brick by Brick." *New York Times*, February 14, 2014.

Selwyn, N. *Should Robots Replace Teachers? AI and the Future of Education*. Medford, MA: Polity Press, 2019.

Shipps, Dorothy. *School Reform, Corporate Style: Chicago 1880–2000*. Lawrence, KS: University of Kansas Press, 2006.

Shore, Cris. "Audit Culture and Illiberal Governance." *Anthropological Theory* 8, no. 3 (2008): 278–298.

Singer, Natasha. "The Silicon Valley Billionaires Remaking America's Schools." *New York Times*, June 6, 2017.

Singer, Natasha, and Mike Isaac. "Mark Zuckerberg's Philanthropy Uses L.L.C. for More Control." *New York Times*, December 2, 2015.

Smarick, Andy. "The Turnaround Fallacy: Stop Trying to Fix Failing Schools. Close Them and Start Fresh." *Education Next* 10, no. 1 (Winter 2010). http://educationnext.org/the-turnaround-fallacy/.

Smyth, Dallas. "On the Audience Commodity and Its Work." In *Dependency Road: Communications, Capitalism, Consciousness, and Canada*. Norwood, NJ: Ablex 1981, 22–51.

Spring, Joel. *Economization of Education*. New York: Routledge, 2015.

Stanley, Jason. *How Fascism Works: The Politics of Us and Them*. New York: Random House, 2018.

Strauss, Valerie. "Big Education Firms Spend Millions Lobbying for Pro-Testing Policies." *Washington Post*, March 30, 2015.

Strauss, Valerie. "Cuomo Questions Why School Buildings Still Exist— and Says New York Will Work with Bill Gates to 'Reimagine Education.'" *Washington Post*, May 6, 2020.

Swami, Viren, and Rebecca Coles. "The Truth Is Out There." *The Psychologist* 23, no. 7 (July 2010). www.thepsychologist.org.uk.

Taylor, Astra. "The Automation Charade." *Logic*, August 1, 2018. https://logicmag.io/failure/the-automation-charade/.

Taylor, Frederick. *The Principles of Scientific Management*. New York: Harper and Brothers, 1911.

Taylor, Keeanga-Yamahta. *From #Blacklivesmatter to Black Liberation.* Chicago: Haymarket Books, 2016.

Tekanji, Blog.shrub.com/check-my-what/. "Check My What? On Privilege and What We Can Do about It," March 8, 2006.

The LEGO Foundation. "Assessing Creativity: A Palette of Possibilities." https://www.legofoundation.com/en/learn-how/knowledge-base /assessing-creativity/.

The LEGO Foundation. "Creating Systems: How Can Education Systems Reform to Enhance Learners' Creativity?" Creativity Matters no. 2. https:// www.legofoundation.com/en/why-play/skills-for-holistic-development /creativity-matters/creativity-matters-report-series/creating-systems/.

The LEGO Foundation. "What We Mean by: Creativity" [leaflet]. https://www.legofoundation.com/en/learn-how/knowledge-base /what-we-mean-by-creativity/.

The Pedagogy of Play Research Team. "Playful Participatory Research: An Emerging Methodology for Developing a Pedagogy of Play." A Project Zero Working Paper [Project Zero at Harvard Graduate School of Education/International School of Billund, Denmark, funded by LEGO Foundation], July 2016. http://www.pz.harvard.edu/resources/playful -participatory-research-an-emerging-methodology-for-developing-a -pedagogy-of-play.

Tiffany, Kaitlyn. "How a Conspiracy Theory about Democrats Drinking Children's Blood Topped Amazon's Best-Sellers List," *Vox,* March 6, 2019. https://www.vox.com/the-goods/2019/3/6/18253505/amazon -qanon-book-best-seller-algorithm-conspiracy.

Tough, Paul. *How Children Succeed: Grit, Curiosity and the Hidden Power of Character.* New York: Houghton-Mifflin, 2012.

Van der Linden, Sander, Costas Panagopoulos, Flavio Azevedo, and John T. Jost. "The Paranoid Style in American Politics Revisited: An Ideological Asymmetry in Conspiratorial Thinking." *Political Psychology* 42, no. 1 (2021): 23–51.

Vaznis, James. "Schools Are Collecting New Data in New Ways about Students with Cutting-Edge High-Tech." *Boston Globe,* December 16, 2019.

https://www.bostonglobe.com/metro/2019/12/16/schools-experiment
-with-high-tech-student-monitoring/7sx3eMEqYTwO9zxzKjyEkK/story
.html.

Williamson, B., J. Pykett, and S. Nemorin. "Biosocial Spaces and Neurocomputational Governance: Brain-Based and Brain-Targeted Technologies in Education." *Discourse: Studies in the Cultural Politics of
Education* 39, no. 2 (2017): 258–275.

Williamson, Ben, and Nelli Piattoeva. "Objectivity as Standardization
in Data-Scientific Education Policy, Technology and Governance."
Learning, Media and Technology 44, no. 1 (2019): 64–76.

Williamson, Ben, and Nelli Piattoeva. "Objectivity as Standardization
in Data-Scientific Education Policy, Technology and Governance," 2018
[author's pre-publication version]. https://www.pure.ed.ac.uk/ws/files
/78326060/WilliamsonB_2018_LMT_Objectivity_standardization.pdf.

Williamson, Ben, Rebecca Enyon, and John Potter. "Pandemic Politics,
Pedagogies and Practices: Digital Technologies and Distance Education during the Coronavirus Emergency." *Learning, Media and Technology,* 45, no. 2 (2020): 107–114. https://doi.org/10.1080/17439884
.2020.1761641.

World Economic Forum. "Schools of the Future: Defining New Models of Education for the Fourth Industrial Revolution." January 2020,
1–33. www.weforum.org.

Wrench in the Gears (blog). "Third Grade Reading Guarantees: Impact
Investors Build System to Terrorize Eight Year Olds." February 27, 2019.
https://wrenchinthegears.com/2019/02/27/3rd-grade-reading-guarantees
-impact-investors-build-system-to-terrorize-eight-year-olds/.

Zizek, Slavoj. *Like a Thief in Broad Daylight.* London: Allen Lane, 2018.

Zuboff, Shoshana. *The Age of Surveillance Capitalism.* New York: Public
Affairs, 2019.

INDEX